the
toddler owner's
manual

D1021881

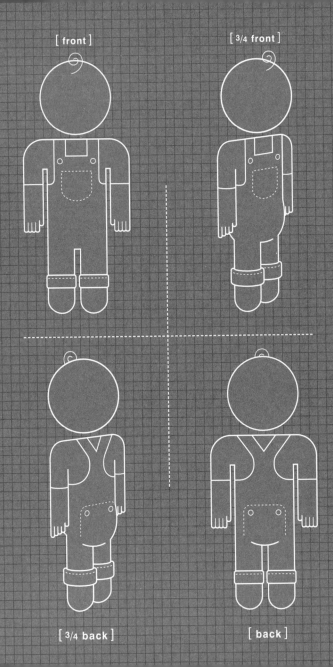

[front]　　　　[3/4 front]

[3/4 back]　　　　[back]

the
toddler
owner's manual

OPERATING INSTRUCTIONS, TROUBLE-SHOOTING
TIPS, AND ADVICE ON SYSTEM MAINTENANCE

by Brett R. Kuhn, Ph.D., and Joe Borgenicht, D.A.D.

Illustrated by Paul Kepple and Jude Buffum

QUIRK BOOKS
PHILADELPHIA

Copyright © 2005 by Quirk Productions, Inc.

Illustrations copyright © 2005 by Headcase Design

All rights reserved. No part of this book may be reproduced in any form
without written permission from the publisher.

Library of Congress Cataloging in Publication Number: 2004195130

ISBN: 1-59474-026-7

Printed in Singapore

Typeset in Swiss

Designed by Paul Kepple and Jude Buffum @ Headcase Design
www.headcasedesign.com

Distributed in North America by Chronicle Books
85 Second Street
San Francisco, CA 94105

10 9 8 7 6 5 4 3 2 1

Quirk Books
215 Church Street
Philadelphia, PA 19106
www.quirkbooks.com

Contents

Upgrading
from Infant to Toddler

VERSION 1.0

VERSION 2.0

Congratulations on your baby's upgrade to "toddler."

Units that have been upgraded to toddler will require frequent bug removal and reprogramming. Though toddler models vary greatly from unit to unit, all toddlers experience phenomenal growth, development, and change and engage in frequent power struggles. *The Toddler Owner's Manual* is a comprehensive user's guide for achieving maximum potential and ensuring optimum operation of your toddler unit. It offers many time-tested programming strategies for the operation of most major updates from ages 1 to 4 years.

It is not necessary to read this manual from cover to cover. Because no two toddlers are exactly alike, this book has been separated into several different sections. Refer to any of the following sections when you experience a problem or have a question that needs to be answered:

UPDATES FOR HOME AND TRANSPORTATION (pages 16–29) describes home upgrades recommended for your toddler unit. It includes useful suggestions for configuring the toddler's room, essential accessories, and required upgrades in transportation equipment.

GENERAL CARE AND HANDLING (pages 30–49) features valuable information about holding, handling, and traveling with the toddler. This section includes a wide array of play skills.

FEEDING: UNDERSTANDING THE TODDLER'S POWER SUPPLY (pages 50–75) provides a valuable guide for understanding and providing the toddler's power supply. It includes information about weaning, recommended diet, and feeding and liquid intake scheduling.

PROGRAMMING SLEEP MODE (pages 76–95) provides an in-depth guide to scheduling and developing the toddler's sleep mode skills. It provides techniques for activating sleep mode, reprogramming sleep mode, transitioning the toddler from a crib to a bed, and trouble-shooting sleeping malfunctions (such as nightmares and night playing).

GENERAL MAINTENANCE AND TRAINING (pages 96–119) is an advanced user's guide to maintaining and training all toddler units for basic physical function and operation. This section includes instructions for training the toddler for self–waste disposal, advanced bathing, and self-dressing.

GROWTH AND DEVELOPMENT (pages 120–151) describes the general characteristics and milestones as toddlers advance their internal odometers. It includes valuable strategies and information on toddlers' physical, verbal, and emotional and social development.

DISCIPLINE (pages 152–177) explores strategies for setting the parameters of a toddler's independent and group functioning. This section also includes techniques for managing a wide array of unwanted behaviors.

SAFETY AND EMERGENCY MAINTENANCE (pages 178–211) describes the best way to toddler-proof the toddler's environment. It includes instructions for performing emergency medical procedures, as well as a short A-to-Z guide to common medical conditions.

Your toddler is experiencing a major upgrade both in external hardware and internal programming as she makes the transition from an infant who is completely dependent on others to a toddler who strives for independence. As your toddler undergoes these changes, you may experience feelings of frustration, incompetence, hopelessness, anger, and despair. These feelings are normal, and with time, they will lessen. With a good sense of humor, you can oversee your toddler's development into a sturdy, self-operational unit.

Good luck—and enjoy your upgraded toddler.

UPGRADE ACCESSORIES (sold separately)

Beverage Delivery System

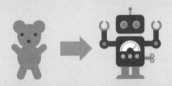

Entertainment Device

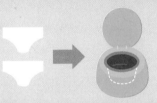

Waste Management

External Casing

Oral Fixation

Mobility Enhancement

Recharging Station

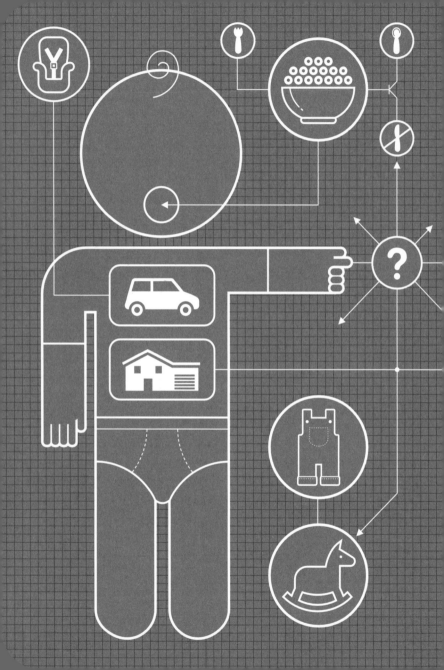

Chapter 1

Updates for Home and Transportation

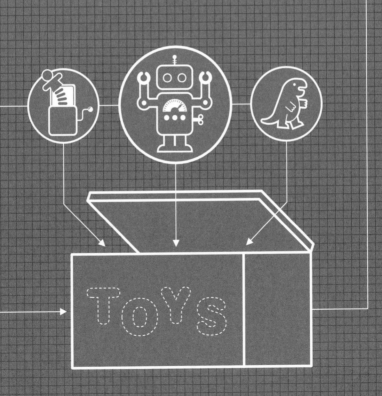

Updating the Home

As a result of a toddler's increased mobility, further toddler-proofing of each room in the home will be necessary to ensure the toddler's safety (see page 180). However, the most involved updating of the home should occur in the room in which the toddler sleeps.

Updating the Toddler's Room

The majority of toddler owners will continue use of a separate sleeping area for their unit (if you practice the operation of co-sleeping, see page 79). This area in the home—previously referred to as a "nursery"— will now be referred to as the "toddler's bedroom." This room should be configured safely (see page 180) and with the following toddler-friendly items to create a secure and comfortable zone for your toddler when she enters self-entertaining and/or sleep modes.

The Toddler Bed: Anywhere between 18 and 36 months following delivery, your toddler will develop the ability to ascend the sides of her crib. When your unit begins this practice, move your toddler into a bed specially de-signed to manage this ability. Toddler beds are typically shorter, narrower, and lower to the ground than standard twin beds. Many toddler beds also come equipped with a rail that runs lengthwise along both sides of the bed to keep the toddler from falling onto the floor. Alternatively, a bed rail may be purchased from a commercial retailer and installed on any bed. See "Trans-ferring the Toddler from a Crib to a Bed" on page 78 for information on placement of the bed and transitioning the toddler from a crib.

Rocker or Chair: Continue use of a rocker or chair if your toddler enjoys the motion and comfort this chair provides. You may replace the full-sized seat with a toddler-sized chair so that your toddler may explore her independence by sitting alone.

⚠ **CAUTION:** *Due to the toddler's increased mobility, use of a changing station may lead to damage of the toddler unit. Remove the changing station entirely or adjust its configuration to a sturdy clothes dresser that is secured firmly to the wall.*

Bookshelves/Books: Shelving units should be attached securely to the wall (see page 181) so the toddler does not pull them down on top of herself. Place heavier items on the lower shelves and lighter items on the upper shelves. Avoid placing breakable items on top of these shelves, as your toddler will develop the ability to climb up and reach them.

Step Stool: This item may be used once your unit has mastered the ability to climb two small steps (usually between the ages of 2 and 3 years) on her own. Place it underneath a light switch so that the toddler can turn her bedroom light on or off when necessary.

Night-Light: Depending on your toddler's ability to operate sleep mode, continued use of a night-light may be required.

Toy Chest/Toys: Toys may be kept in a separate room or placed in a container under the toddler bed or off to one side of the room. Do not store heavy toys off the ground or on high shelves.

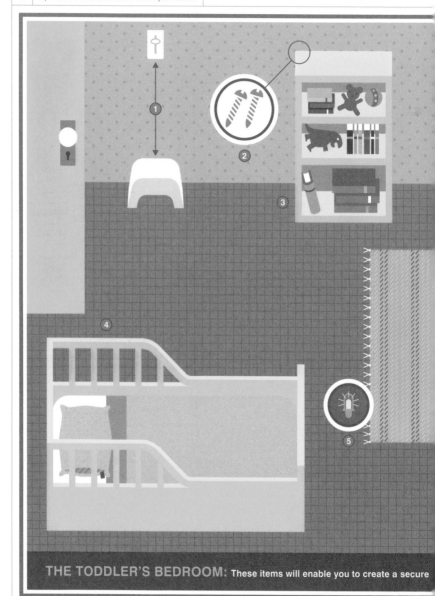

THE TODDLER'S BEDROOM: These items will enable you to create a secure

1. Step stool to reach light switch
2. Bookshelf attached securely to wall
3. Keep heaviest items on bottom shelf
4. Bed with rail on either side
5. Night-light
6. Rocking horse
7. Toy chest
8. Toddler-sized chair
9. Educational toys
10. Encourage creativity

and comfortable zone for your toddler to enter self-entertaining and/or sleep modes.

Toddler Accessories

As your toddler upgrades from an infant, you will be required to secure a broad array of additional accessories for dressing, cleaning, sleeping, fueling, and entertaining the unit. You may already have many of these supplies in stock. However, due to your toddler's natural growth and development, these accessories must be upgraded regularly in size and configuration as needed.

SLEEPING SUPPLIES

- 3–4 sets fitted toddler bedsheets
- 2 rubber mattress covers
- 2 blankets
- 1 small, firm pillow with 2 cases

TOILET TRAINING SUPPLIES

- 1 toilet training seat and/or 1 toilet training potty
- 6–12 pairs of absorbent toddler underpants and/or 3–6 pairs of lined absorbent toddler underpants

CLOTHING SUPPLIES

- 2–3 one-piece undershirts
- 5–7 long-sleeved shirts
- 5–7 T-shirts
- 5–7 pairs of pants
- 5–7 pairs of shorts
- 2–3 dresses
  (optional, for female units)
- 5–7 pairs of socks
- 1–3 sweaters or sweatshirts
- 1 raincoat (as needed)
- 1 winter coat (as needed)
- 1–2 pairs of shoes
- 1 pair of mittens
- 1 winter hat
- 1 brimmed summer hat

FEEDING SUPPLIES

- 4–6 sippy cups and/or 4–6 plastic toddler cups
- 2–3 sets toddler plastic ware (plate and bowl)
- 2 sets plastic toddler utensils
- 2 plastic place mats
- 1 highchair and/or booster chair
- 1 plastic under-chair spill mat

CLEANING SUPPLIES

- 1 toddler-soft toothbrush
- 1 tube toddler-safe toothpaste
- 1 bottle toddler soap
- 1 bottle toddler-safe shampoo
- 1 hairbrush

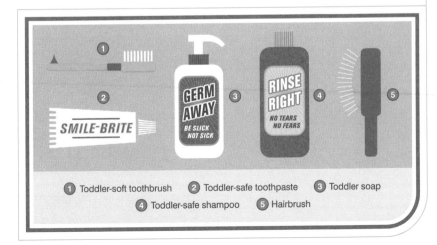

1 Toddler-soft toothbrush 2 Toddler-safe toothpaste 3 Toddler soap 4 Toddler-safe shampoo 5 Hairbrush

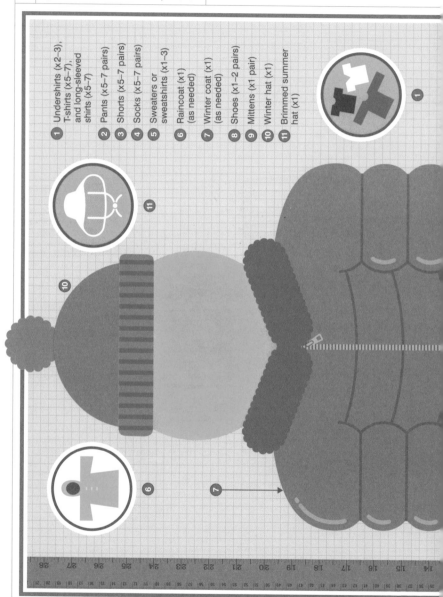

1. Undershirts (x2–3), T-shirts (x5–7), and long-sleeved shirts (x5–7)
2. Pants (x5–7 pairs)
3. Shorts (x5–7 pairs)
4. Socks (x5–7 pairs)
5. Sweaters or sweatshirts (x1–3)
6. Raincoat (x1) (as needed)
7. Winter coat (x1) (as needed)
8. Shoes (x1–2 pairs)
9. Mittens (x1 pair)
10. Winter hat (x1)
11. Brimmed summer hat (x1)

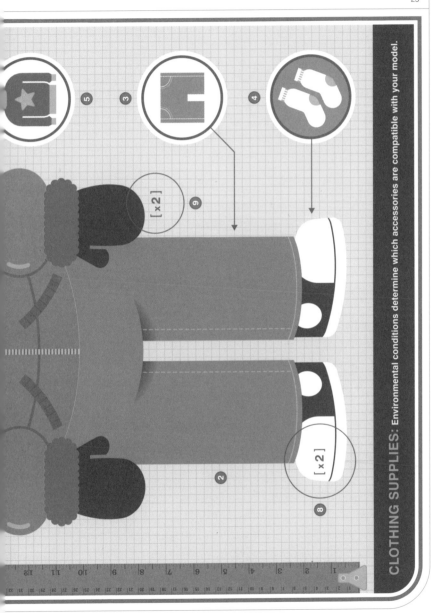

25

CLOTHING SUPPLIES: Environmental conditions determine which accessories are compatible with your model.

Transportation Updates

As a former baby owner, you will already have some accessories to aid in the transportation of your toddler unit. However, in some cases, your toddler's physical development will necessitate an update of many of these items.

⚠ *CAUTION: Continued use of infant-model carriers and car seats (in particular) is satisfactory as long as your toddler remains within the height and weight standards recommended by the manufacturer. If your toddler has outgrown these items, discontinue use immediately and replace them with an appropriately rated device.*

Car Seats

Toddlers should continue to be transported in a car seat placed on the rear seat of your vehicle (preferably in the center of the seat). Many toddler car seats may be used in either rear- or forward-facing positions; however, do not place your toddler in a forward-facing position until she reaches minimum age and weight specifications (generally 1 year following delivery and a weight of 20 pounds [9 kg]).

Tethered Car Seats (Fig. A): A tethered car seat resembles an infant/ toddler convertible seat. It may be used according to height and weight specifications listed by the manufacturer, most commonly between the ages of 1 and 4 years. Most tethered car seats include a five-point harness, adjustable seat belt, and padding. Additionally, a tether that runs from the top of the car seat may be clipped into a properly secured bolt or hook in the rear of the vehicle. This tether will provide additional safety by fixing the car seat to a more permanent feature in the vehicle.

CAR SEATS

(Fig. A)
TETHERED CAR SEAT

1 For ages 1 to 4 years

2 Five-point harness

3 External tether provides additional safety

4 Adjustable seat belt

5 Consult manufacturer's height and weight specifications

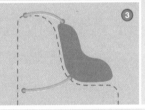

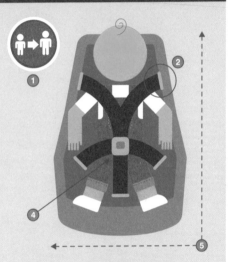

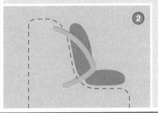

(Fig. B)
BOOSTER SEAT

1 For ages 4 years and older

2 Utilizes existing seat belt

3 Belt rests across hips and chest (not abdomen and neck)

4 Consult manufacturer's height and weight specifications

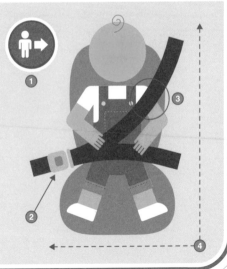

⚠ **EXPERT TIP:** *Many newer cars, trucks, and vans come with a tether anchor built into the vehicle. If your vehicle does not have a firm, factory in-stalled tether, visit your local auto dealer and ask that they properly install an aftermarket anchor.*

Booster Seats (Fig. B): A booster seat looks like an infant/toddler con-vertible seat without the base. Boosters fit on the car's seat and are affixed most commonly by a seat belt once the toddler is in place. Such seats should generally be put to use when the toddler reaches 4 years of age and weighs 40 pounds (18 kg). Additionally, the booster should be used with belts that rest across the toddler's hips and chest, rather than the abdomen and neck.

Wheeled Vehicles

In addition to strollers, several different types of wheeled vehicles may be employed to transport a toddler on sidewalks, through shopping centers, and anywhere else the child refuses to use his own feet to walk.

WHEELED VEHICLES

Model: DOUBLE STROLLER

Wheels: 4 to 8

Steering: Toddler owner

Helmet: Optional, at toddler owner's discretion

Operation: Pushed by toddler owner

Recommendation for use: Best for all-around transport of multiple units (siblings, friends, etc.)

Model: TRICYCLE

Wheels: 3

Steering: Either toddler or toddler owner (many models include a wheel lock and "driving bar" that allow steering to be controlled by either operator)

Helmet: Required

Operation: Pedaled or pushed along ground by foot, or owner pushed

Recommendation for use: Best on sidewalks when accompanied by toddler owner for proper supervision

Model: WAGON

Wheels: 4

Steering: Toddler owner

Helmet: Optional, at toddler owner's discretion (recommended for low-sided or open-back wagons)

Operation: Pushed or pulled by toddler owner

Recommendation for use: Best in grocery stores, shopping centers, or on sidewalks. Pull wagon behind you as you walk. Be sure to check toddler frequently to ensure that he is seated safely in the wagon.

Chapter 2

General Care and Handling

Handling and Holding the Toddler

The toddler's physical development will allow the user to handle the unit in new ways; however, care must still be taken when operating the unit. Frequent washing of the hands is recommended, but as the unit approaches her second year of operation and subsequently her immune system strengthens, such practice is not as necessary.

Picking Up the Toddler

A toddler's increased neck and back strength will allow you to pick her up in a more casual manner than when she was an infant.

⚠ *CAUTION: A toddler's bones, joints, ligaments, and sockets will continue to develop for some time. Thus, a toddler should always be picked up from underneath both armpits. Never lift or drag your unit by the arms or legs. Temporary but recurring appendage malfunction may occur.*

[1] Insert both hands under the armpits of the toddler (between the arm and the body).

[2] Gently grasp the toddler with a solid but moderate grip.

[3] Lift the toddler directly upward and bring the unit closer to your own body to aid in support.

[4] Hold on one hip, or employ another hold, as detailed below.

⚠️ **EXPERT TIP:** *As your toddler approaches 25 to 30 pounds (11–14 kg), lift the toddler using your legs rather than your back. Bend at the knees, grasp the toddler as above, and stand up using your leg muscles.*

The On-the-Shoulder Hold (Fig. A)

This hold is recommended for heavier toddlers and longer distances. Many toddlers will not like this hold initially, as it puts them much higher off the ground than they are used to.

⚠️ **CAUTION:** *Be aware when walking through doorways or under trees with a toddler on your shoulder. You may need to dip slightly down when passing under low objects.*

[1] Face the toddler away from you and pick her up under her armpits.

[2] Raise the toddler up and over your head.

[3] Seat her firmly on your neck so that her legs straddle your neck and her belly rests on the back of your head.

[4] Instruct the toddler to hold onto you by wrapping her arms around your head, by grasping your forehead, or if the toddler's arms are long enough, by wrapping them under your chin.

[5] Place both of your hands over your head and onto the back of your toddler to hold her in place as you walk. Alternatively, when the toddler learns to hold on firmly, you may secure the toddler in place by grasping her feet as you walk.

(Fig. A)
ON-THE-SHOULDER HOLD

1. Stand behind the toddler
2. Bend your knees and reach under the toddler's arms
3. Raise the toddler up and over your head
4. Seat the toddler firmly on your neck, wrapping your arms around his back
5. WARNING: Be aware of low objects like doorways

(Fig. B)
PIGGYBACK HOLD

1. Kneel in front of toddler
2. Have the toddler wrap his arms around your neck
3. Wrapping both arms around the toddler, lean forward at a 45-degree angle
4. Continue leaning forward as you stand up
5. WARNING: Be aware of low objects like doorways

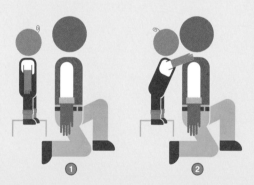

HANDLING THE TODDLER: Utilize the On-the-Shoulder Hold when

traveling long distances and the Piggyback Hold for shorter trips.

The Piggyback Hold (Fig. B)

Use the Piggyback Hold during playtimes or for short-distance travel.

[1] Kneel down in front of the toddler with the toddler facing your back.

[2] Instruct the toddler to wrap her arms around your neck. Wrap your own arms behind you and around the toddler's rear end.

[3] With your arms around and underneath the toddler, lean forward to a 45-degree angle. Pull the toddler's body to your own so that the toddler straddles your back.

[4] Lean forward as you stand, supporting the toddler from below.

Comforting the Toddler

One of the main characteristics of all toddler models is their simultaneous quest for independence and need for security. As a result of this contradiction in early toddler programming, your unit may require frequent comfort from you as she develops the ability to self-soothe. Many toddlers will display visual cues (pouting, tears) and audio cues (crying, whining) to communicate the need for comfort. Use the following techniques to comfort your toddler and to install a sturdy bond between toddler and owner.

Head Stroking: Run your fingers back and forth and in circular motions on the toddler's head while reading books, installing pajamas, interfacing with the television, and any time the toddler requires comfort. Head stroking can also act as positive reinforcement when your toddler exhibits appropriate behavior.

Cuddling: Many toddlers enjoy cuddling, or close holding and affection, while some dislike the feeling of confinement. In general, cuddling with your toddler may help her to feel safe and secure.

⚠️ *EXPERT TIP: Allow the toddler to move freely while cuddling—do not place restrictions or schedule cuddling only during specific time periods. Such freedom will help to install the executable program for self-soothing.*

Lobe Rubbing: Gently pinch the lobe of your toddler's auditory receptors between your thumb and forefinger. Move your thumb and finger in a circular motion. This action may help a toddler to enter sleep mode or temporarily freeze the toddler's operating system.

Singing: From infancy, your toddler can absorb the sounds and rhythms of musical programming. When coupled with the tone of an owner's voice, song can add another layer of ease to any toddler's tumultuous operations.

Praising the Toddler

Unlabeled praise is a nonspecific statement that makes your toddler feel good (e.g., "wow" or "good job!"). Your toddler may appreciate the positive attention, but he will be unclear as to why he received it.

Use labeled praise, a specific statement that indicates both your approval and the reason for your approval, to reinforce your toddler's acceptable behaviors. Use specifics, such as "Thank you for using your indoor voice," to help the toddler attach your praise to a specific behavior.

Playing with the Toddler

Playing with your toddler promotes attachment and a positive owner-toddler relationship. Playing helps to upgrade all the functions of a toddler's programming, including verbal skills, physical coordination, social interfacing, and emotional health. Note that it is not the specific activity (visiting the zoo, playing in the sand, and so forth) that programs attachment and bonding; rather, the bond is formed through the character of the owner-toddler interactions that transpire during the activity.

Toddler-Directed Interaction

Use the following guidelines during structured playtimes to increase your unit's independence and strengthen the bond between you.

[1] Enter your toddler's world of imagination and play. Allow him to be in charge as you follow his lead (except when he is leading toward dangerous or negative behaviors).

[2] Allow your toddler to decide where to sit or what to play with. Resist the urge to instruct your toddler on the proper way to do something.

[3] Allow your toddler to direct the conversation, if any. Do not ask leading questions, like "What are you doing now?" or "Are you going to color?"

[4] Do not correct your toddler's actions ("That doesn't go there"). Encourage him to explore his environment through play, trial and error, and problem solving.

[5] Act excited, enthusiastic, and even silly. Do not be afraid to behave in a childlike manner.

[6] Praise appropriate behavior. Frequent use of positive reinforcement will help to program the toddler's good behavior. His internal processors will take note of the cause (cleaning up toys) and effect (your praise) of his good behavior. Most toddlers will strive for this effect in the future.

[7] Make frequent physical contact. Touch your toddler often for one- or two-second intervals. Place your arm around your toddler's shoulders, deliver a brief hug or kiss, or gently stroke your toddler's hair, face, or the back of his neck to indicate your love and approval.

[8] Verbally describe your toddler's behavior to focus his attention and thoughts. Additionally, such attention may produce a calming effect.

[9] Imitate appropriate behavior to send the message that you approve of your unit's activity. Imitation may also promote sharing.

[10] Repeat or paraphrase what your child says. This activity will improve a toddler's speech and language skills.

⚠ **CAUTION:** *The above skills are designed to increase your toddler's appropriate behavior. Do not use them in response to inappropriate behavior. If your child is behaving inappropriately, refer to Chapter 7: Discipline.*

Music and Dance

Both music and dance may be used as play activities. In addition to entertainment, these procedures help with the installation of a toddler's rhythm, repetition, language, organization, instruction, and spatial awareness programming. Use the following strategies when playing music, singing, or dancing with your toddler.

[1] Sing songs that have a simple structure, steady beat, and easy repetition in both music and lyrics.

[2] Use hand movements to illustrate the lyrics of a song. Many toddlers will perform the hand movements even before they know how to sing.

[3] Allow the toddler to experiment with musical instruments. Let the toddler explore and discover an instrument's many forms of making sound.

[4] When dancing or playing instruments, practice playing or dancing, suddenly stopping, and then playing or dancing again. The toddler may enjoy the challenge of anticipation and will focus his attention intently on you and the music. This exercise will also promote his feelings of physical control over his body.

[5] Teach your toddler both repetitious dance steps as well as the freedom to create his own. Some toddler owners will choreograph steps and then mirror their toddler's steps. This activity will help to develop your toddler's organizational skills as well as his creativity.

Toy Accessories

The use of age-appropriate toy accessories is vital to your toddler's physical and cognitive development. Pay attention to specifications for use when purchasing toys for your toddler—note the manufacturer's recommendations on the minimum age requirement for use of a particular item. Your toddler's limited comprehension of danger makes it important that you avoid supplying her with toys that have sharp edges or loose or small parts.

⚠ *EXPERT TIP: Despite the immense range of manufactured toys for all levels of toddler models, some of the best (and least expensive) toddler toys are basic household items. For example, a box filled with tissue paper and wrapped in a box with a ribbon may suffice as a gift for a toddler. Other safe and effective household items that can be used as toys include toilet paper/paper towel rolls, wooden spoons, spatulas, metal pots and pans, coasters, and plastic containers.*

Toys for Toddlers Age 12 to 24 Months

Push and Pull Toys: Once your toddler has mastered the ability to walk, push and pull toys will allow her to practice this skill.

Balls: Any ball larger than your toddler's mouth will aid in teaching her a number of different skills. Small, soft balls may be used for catching or throwing. Medium-sized balls may be used for grasping or kicking. Large balls may be used for pushing, bouncing, or chasing.

Blocks or Building Bricks: Blocks and bricks will allow your toddler to practice fine motor skills by stacking, cognitive skills by sorting, and creative skills by building.

Picture and Board Books: Your toddler will enjoy books that allow her to follow simple stories and recognize shapes, colors, numbers, and letters. Most units are most stimulated by books that are colorful and allow tactile stimulation and movement (i.e., pop-up books). Board books will allow her to "read" independently. Toddlers enjoy repetition, so be prepared to read and reread the same books for several days at a time. Purchase a few small books that will fit easily in your toddler's crib or bed to promote self-entertaining.

Art Supplies: Stamps with washable inks, chalk, nontoxic play dough, or washable paints, crayons, and markers will allow your toddler to create. Your toddler will develop the ability to scribble with these items on a piece of paper or other markable surface. An easel or a table will allow your toddler to explore her artistic side and confine her artistic messes.

Cars, Trucks, Trains: These toys, as long as they are somewhat large and well built, without small parts, will allow your toddler to work on her fine motor skills. Toy train sets, construction sites, or gas station parking lots will also challenge your toddler to make believe and act out stories.

Dolls, Dollhouses: Dolls and dollhouses—with well-built, nonbreakable parts—allow your toddler to use her imagination. She will act out various familial situations, which may give you some insight into her emotions. Larger dolls that are easier to handle and contain large moving parts will work your unit's fine motor skills and help her learn to operate clothing (i.e., zippers, buttons, ties, and the like).

Instruments: Musical instruments of all kinds will allow your toddler to explore her own musical programming as well as teach her cause and effect. Use toddler-designed instruments, generally plastic with easily manageable parts, such as rattles, kazoos, and bells. Actual woodwind, brass, or stringed instruments are not recommended for this age group.

Riding Toys: Low, three- or four-wheeled ride-on vehicles will give your toddler the opportunity to test her coordination and balance.

Digging Toys: Shovels, buckets, rakes, and sifters should be used to introduce the toddler to sand or dirt. These toys encourage self-entertainment.

Toys for Toddlers Age 2 to 3 Years

As the toddler approaches her third year of operation, continue use of the above-listed toys, in addition to more complex toys, such as these:

Construction and Building Bricks: Building sets will challenge your toddler's ability to sort, follow instructions, and build objects. The smaller parts in some of these sets require that your toddler be age 3 or older, so consult the manufacturer's age recommendation before purchasing.

Puzzles: Models who put together puzzles function more effectively in the subjects of math, spelling, and science later in life. Start your toddler with simple puzzles—6 to 12 pieces—and then expand her horizons to more complex challenges, like puzzles of 24 to 64 pieces.

Games: Many 2- and 3-year-old toddlers enjoy playing with board games. Memorization and puzzle games are recommended for this age group.

Sports Equipment: Virtually every type of sporting equipment is available in a size appropriate for toddler play. Plastic bats and balls, foam footballs, plastic basketballs, and so forth, will teach the toddler physical skills.

FOR USE AT 12–24 MONTHS

1. Riding toys
2. Art supplies
3. Cars, trucks, and trains
4. Push and pull toys
5. Dolls
6. Digging toys
7. Picture and board books
8. Instruments

UPGRADES AT 2–3 YEARS

9. Building blocks
10. Sports equipment
11. Puzzles
12. Memory games

TOY ACCESSORIES: The use of age-appropriate accessories (sold

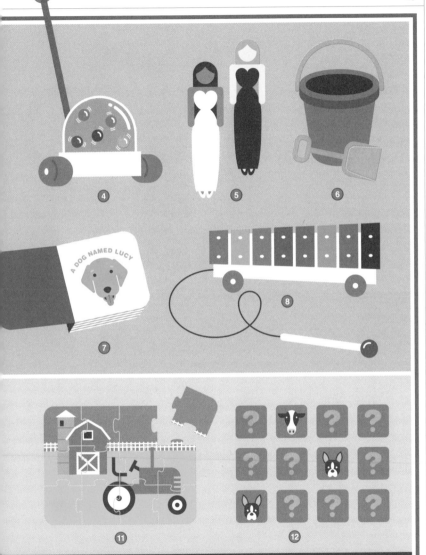

separately) are vital to your model's physical and cognitive development.

Traveling with the Toddler

Use the following strategies to entertain and travel safely with your toddler.

Traveling by Car

When traveling with your toddler by car, strategies depend entirely upon the length of the trip. Your primary challenge when traveling greater distances (more than an hour) is keeping the toddler from getting bored. Carry plenty of books, small toys, music, food, and drink to help entertain the toddler. Additionally, plan on making pit stops every 1 to 2 hours (depending on your toddler's state of mind). Get out of the car and stretch, and play for about 15 minutes at a time.

⚠ *CAUTION: Never take the toddler out of his car seat while you are driving. Always come to a complete stop before removing the toddler from his seat.*

Traveling by Airplane

When traveling by airplane with your toddler, you may be dealing with any range of preprogrammed emotions, including excitement, boredom, and anxiety. The longer the flight, the more likely you will have temporary outbursts to contend with. Consider the length of your flight and adjust your strategies accordingly.

Preparing for Travel

[1] Book your flight with your toddler's sleep schedule in mind. You may choose to fly at night so your toddler may sleep through most of the flight.

AIR TRANSPORT

TIPS FOR AIR TRAVEL

1. Groom model for optimal passenger compliance
2. Fly at night for peace and quiet
3. Install I.D. bracelet on model
4. Bringing the model's car seat offers added protection and comfort
5. Secure bulkhead seats for maximum space

SUPPLIES LIST

6. Diapers (bring twice the estimated amount)
7. Change of clothes
8. Healthy snacks
9. Beverages
10. Toys (bring favorites along with new ones)

However, if your toddler doesn't fall asleep, he will be even more tired and irritable.

[2] Fly nonstop, but during off-peak times. A midweek flight during the middle of the day is more likely to have open seats that will allow you to stretch out and provide more free space for your active toddler.

[3] Check with your travel agent or airline to see if you can reserve the bulkhead, or front row, seats. These seats provide extra floor space and allow the toddler more room to move.

EXPERT TIP: *Many airlines hold bulkhead seats until the day or even the hour of departure. Ask the attendant at the gate for the best seats possible.*

[4] Consider taking a car seat for your toddler to sit in on the plane. The seat can provide protection in case of turbulence, and your toddler will be in a familiar seat where he is accustomed to sitting for long periods, making him more likely to be better behaved and to fall asleep.

[5] Plan for flight delays and layovers. Pack twice as many diapers and wipes as you think you'll need, as well as an extra set of clothing and snacks.

[6] Take a variety of snacks on the plane with you. Pack a small plastic container full of dry cereal, cheese sticks, crackers, cookies, and fruit snacks. Also bring an assortment of liquids.

[7] Pack enough small, quiet toys to keep your toddler interested and busy. Bring a few favorite toys and books, as well as brand-new items that you can introduce on the plane.

Day of Departure

[1] Groom your toddler before the trip. Fellow passengers will be more sympathetic and willing to help you if your toddler is clean and cute.

[2] Place an identifying bracelet on your toddler. Tag your toddler's wrist with your name, destination, flight number, home address, and home phone and cell phone numbers.

[3] Allow your child to expend energy before boarding the plane. Walk from the parking lot to the terminal, and take him for a walk around the airport.

[4] Review the rules of the plane with your toddler before you arrive at the airport, when you enter, and again as you prepare to board. Some rules may include no kicking the seats, use an indoor voice, no jumping or running, and remain in the seat with a seat belt on when the seat belt sign is lit.

[5] If you are traveling with another toddler owner, split up when the airline announces its preboarding procedures. One can enter the plane to secure the carry-on luggage and the car seat. The other can remain off the plane with the toddler to keep him moving around and occupied. Board the toddler at last call.

EXPERT TIP: Cabin pressure changes with the altitude during take off and landing, placing unequal pressure on your toddler's ears. Chewing gum, sucking on a lollipop or a pacifier, or drinking juice from a sippy cup or straw may help alleviate the pressure.

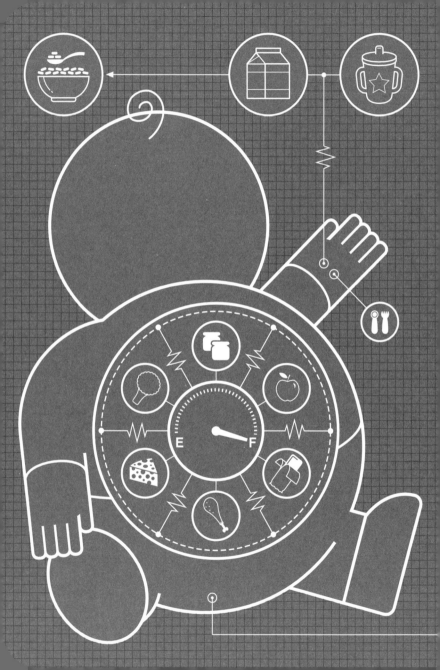

Chapter 3

Feeding: Understanding the Toddler's Power Supply

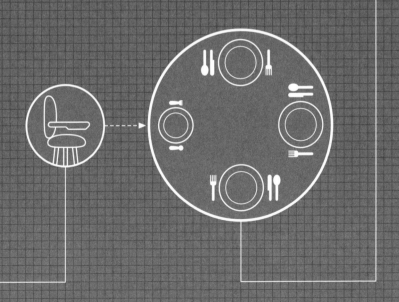

Weaning from Breast- or Bottle-Feeding

"Weaning" refers to the process of transitioning the toddler from breast- or bottle-feeding to drinking from a cup. There is no prescribed right time for weaning—the process can be started when both mother and toddler are ready. Many toddlers are ready to make this transition once their pincer grasp has fully developed and they are self-feeding with finger foods.

Self-Weaning

Some toddler users desire a more active approach to weaning, while others prefer to wait for the toddler to self-wean. If you prefer to allow your toddler to self-wean, stop offering the breast or bottle, but do not refuse it when he asks for it. Gradually, your toddler will stop asking, though the total amount of time this process will take varies from model to model.

Active Weaning

[1] Fill a sippy cup with a small portion of your toddler's preferred nutritious drink (breast milk, formula, whole cow's milk). Initially use a spout with open holes, or take out the spill-proof insert so that it is easier for the toddler to learn to suck the spout.

⚠ *CAUTION: Do not introduce more than one change at a time. Fill a newly introduced cup with a familiar and preferred drink (formula, whole milk, expressed breast milk). Wait to change the type of liquid until after your toddler has adjusted to the new intake method.*

[2] Splash a bit of liquid on the spout and gently tip it into her mouth to give her a taste of what's inside. Provide hand-over-hand physical guidance if necessary, but don't force-feed. Your toddler may play with her sippy cup before using it for its intended purpose.

EXPERT TIP: Purchase several types of sippy cups to allow your toddler to experiment and find her favorite type before purchasing a number of them. Most offer a spill-proof snap-on or screw-on lid. Younger toddlers will prefer a cup with two handles and a rounded, weighted bottom to keep it upright.

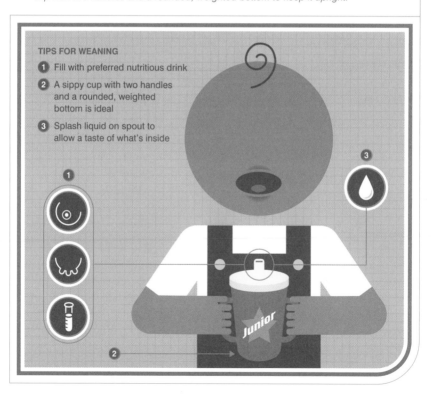

[3] When your toddler is familiar, comfortable, and skilled with the new intake method, make drinking from the sippy cup more desirable and breast- or bottle-feeding less desirable. Do not allow your toddler to have a bottle except at mealtime. Put a bit more fluid in the cup and less fluid in the bottle. Gradually dilute bottle formula with more and more water. Put your toddler's preferred liquids (breast milk, formula, whole milk) in the sippy cup and less-preferred liquids in the bottle.

[4] Offer a sippy cup first thing in the morning and just before regular feeding times, when your toddler is most interested and hungry. Postpone a breast- or bottle-feeding session for a short time or until after a meal or snack, when the toddler is more likely to be full from eating finger foods.

[5] Gradually eliminate breast- or bottle-feedings, removing another feeding every two weeks. Begin by replacing the midday feeding, then the late afternoon, morning, and finally the bedtime breast- or bottle-feeding.

[6] Shorten each nighttime breast- or bottle-feeding session before stopping completely. Make sure the child is still awake when each feeding ends.

*⚠ **EXPERT TIP:** If your toddler actively resists the weaning process, she may be depending upon breast- or bottle-feeding for comfort rather than just as a power supply. Find alternative ways to meet these needs. Continue to hold, rock, and sing to your toddler without feeding.*

Fuel Requirement Guidelines

The toddler's power supply is provided by the food he eats and beverages he drinks. Use the guidelines below as general parameters when feeding your own unit.

Basic Nutrition Requirements

Many owners overestimate how much food their toddler should consume. Because her physical growth has slowed down, a 2-year-old toddler may actually eat less than a 9-month-old baby. Most toddler models are able to survive and even thrive on what appears to be no food. In fact, a 2-year-old model really only needs eight to nine bites of food per meal.

As a general rule, a toddler only needs to consume between 900 and 1,200 calories each day (about 46 calories for each pound [102 calories for each kg] your toddler weighs). This works out to a surprisingly little amount of food. For each meal, toddlers should have 1 tablespoon of food per year of age from several food groups. For example, a 3-year-old toddler should consume 3 tablespoons of food from each of two to three food groups during each meal. Many toddlers will stretch this amount over several meals—eating a few bites at one sitting and making up the difference at another. This process may even be stretched out over several hours or even days.

Do not put too much emphasis on your toddler's eating. It is an owner's responsibility to provide healthy meals, and a toddler's responsibility to decide how much she will eat during each meal.

⚠️ **CAUTION:** *Do not get caught up in counting your toddler's calories. The food your toddler eats over the course of several weeks or months is more important than the food she eats in a single meal or even in an entire day. Studies have shown that toddlers have an inborn ability to eat the right amount of calories and nutrients they need to survive when they are given a variety of healthful food options. If you are concerned that your toddler isn't getting enough vitamins or minerals, consult your toddler's service provider to see if a children's vitamin is recommended.*

The Nutritional Pyramid

Much research has been done to determine healthy amounts of food, from different food groups, that every toddler model will thrive on. Use the following chart to institute healthy daily standards of your own:

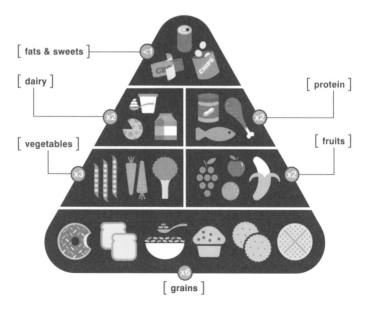

Grains

Toddlers require five to six daily servings of grains. Whole wheat breads are more beneficial than white breads, and hydrogenated oil–free crackers are more healthy than those with hydrogenated oils. Grains include breads, pastas, crackers, cereals, oatmeal, and rice.

Fruits and Vegetables

Serve two to three servings of fruits and two to three servings of vegetables daily. Some toddlers will take to a particular vegetable or fruit, but continue to introduce new items from this group to keep them interested and to vary their intake. Many units dislike the skins of fruits, such as apples or peaches. The fiber found in whole fruits and vegetables make it worthwhile to offer as many as you can.

Dairy

Limit a toddler's daily dairy consumption to the equivalent of two to three 8- to 12-ounce (237–355 ml) servings of milk. At around 12 months, toddlers usually supplement or switch entirely from formula or breast milk to whole cow's milk. Some toddlers take to cow's milk quickly, while others may need added preparation—including warming or a chocolate additive. The latter, in particular, is recommended in moderation. Other foods that provide a toddler with dairy nutrition include yogurt, ice cream, and cheese.

⚠ *CAUTION: Consult your service provider if the toddler is consuming more or less of the recommended daily allowance of dairy. The service provider may recommend switching to 2 percent or skim milk to prevent overfeeding, or a calcium supplement to ensure that he is receiving the required amount.*

Proteins

Toddlers require two to four servings of proteins each day. Limit each serving to 1 to 2 ounces (28–57 g) and offer lean, low-fat meat. Proteins include eggs, meats, fish, soy products (tofu), peanut butter, and beans.

Foods to Limit

Some foods, such as popcorn, hot dogs, and peanuts (see chart on page 59), present a choking hazard and should be avoided completely until the toddler is at least 4 years old. Other foods, such as honey or peanut butter, may cause an allergic reaction in some models. Limit your toddler's access to—and thus intake of—the following:

■ *Fast food.* Offer fast food once a week or less. These foods may promote habitual eating of high-calorie/low-nutrient foods.
■ *Candy.* Offer candy on special occasions, once or twice a week, or as part of an occasional meal. Never give a toddler hard round candy, as it may cause choking.
■ *Dessert.* Offer dessert a few times a week, or make dessert nutritious, such as yogurt or fruit.

CHOKING HAZARDS: Do not serve your toddler food that is thick and sticky, tough, round, or hard. Properly prepare (or otherwise avoid) the following until your toddler is 4 years old:

- Caramels
- Chewing gum
- Hot dogs (unless cut lengthwise into thin strips)
- Uncrushed ice cubes
- Large fatty pieces of meat
- Nuts or seeds
- Popcorn
- Raw carrots
- Raw celery
- Raw peas
- Whole grapes

Liquid Intake Options

All toddlers require the use of beverages for proper growth and hydration. Many units may also use extra fluid to wash down foods during mealtimes.

One of the most effective techniques to teach toddlers consumption of healthy beverages is modeling. The more an owner consumes healthy beverages like milk or water during the day and at mealtimes, the more likely a toddler is to consume the same. Consider providing your toddler with the following beverages.

WHOLE

2%

Milk

Present cow's milk to your toddler as an option after 1 year of age. Whole milk should be used until the toddler is at least 2 years old. After that, you may use 2 percent or skim milk—depending on family preference. As a general rule, your toddler should consume at least 16 ounces (473 ml) of milk (or other dairy products; see page 57) per day.

Soy, rice, or other substitute milks may be served once your toddler reaches age 2, so long as the liquid is fortified. Cow's milk is more nutrient dense and is recommended over substitute milks unless your child has an allergy.

Water

Your toddler should consume 1 to 2 cups (1.5 ounces per pound [100 ml per kilo]) of water per day to remain hydrated. If your toddler has problems gaining weight, she should consume whole milk rather than water throughout the day.

Juices

Juice is the subject of much debate among toddler nutrition experts. Too much intake of this liquid may cause diarrhea and contribute to weight problems. Juice is also low in nutrients and is generally sweetened with additional sugar, so it may assist in developing a toddler's attraction to sugar and cause her to feel prematurely full.

Your toddler should consume no more than 2 to 4 ounces (59–118 ml) of juice per day. You may begin the day with juice, and then move to milk and water through dinner.

Juice Weaning

If your toddler drinks more juice than is recommended and refuses other beverages, use the following procedure to limit your toddler's juice intake and increase her water intake.

[1] Serve a small amount of juice in the morning.

[2] Fill a sippy cup with half juice and half water in the daytime.

[3] Fill a cup consisting of one-quarter (or less) juice and three-quarters water in the evening.

[4] Do not allow your toddler to walk away from the table with juice. Tell her she must stay at the table to finish her cup.

Beverages to Avoid

Limit your toddler's access to soda, fruit juices, punches, and flavored milks to special occasions and celebrations. Caffeinated beverages should be avoided completely until the toddler is at least 2 years old.

Programming the Toddler's Feeding Schedule

Most toddlers will eat three meals and two snacks per day. Meals include breakfast in the morning, lunch in the early afternoon, and dinner in the evening. Snacks can occur between meals, and sometimes just before bed if your toddler seems especially hungry. When programming the toddler's feeding schedule, use the following strategies.

EXPERT TIP: *Preparing food in a toddler-friendly manner is essential to your toddler's eating success. Present your toddler's foods in small, quarter-inch (0.5 cm) pieces to avoid choking. Cook (or slightly overcook) your toddler's foods, as many prefer soft foods to aid in chewing. Some toddler models prefer to have their food separated by type. Many toddlers find the mixing or touching of foods on their plates to be unpalatable.*

[1] Schedule your toddler's breakfast, lunch, and dinner at the same time that you eat so that you can introduce appropriate mealtime behavior and pass on a healthy attitude toward a variety of foods.

[2] Keep meals healthful and full of variety. Offer at least two or three different food options (for example, one serving of turkey, one serving of vegetables, and one serving of potatoes or French fries).

[3] When feeding your toddler, make it a goal to set her eating pattern now to give her the best opportunity to avoid eating issues later in life.

[4] Set reasonable goals. It is normal for toddlers' appetites to vary from day to day. A reasonable short-term goal is to make mealtime pleasant and

free of conflict. A long-term goal is to teach your toddler to eat a variety of foods, and to be able to do so in social situations.

[5] Do not allow your toddler to "graze," a condition in which toddlers eat a little bit all day long. Avoid using food as pacification, such as handing your toddler a snack when she fusses or whines. Constant snacking will affect your toddler's eating habits and ability to eat well during scheduled meals. Toddlers who graze tend to consume more junk food and take in fewer calories than those who eat on a schedule.

[6] Choose a consistent location to eat. The location will serve as a signal for your toddler to know when it is time to eat. Without consistency, your toddler may confuse playing and eating.

[7] Ask for an older toddler's input while shopping or preparing food. This will give the toddler some control over what she gets to eat but will not put too much emphasis on her success or failure when it comes time to do so.

[8] Don't give up on a newly introduced food item just because the toddler uses her audio system to express displeasure. Toddlers may require 10 to 20 exposures to a new food item before they get accustomed to the color, shape, smell, and texture. Be patient with this process, and praise your toddler for taking a taste of food, even if she spits it back out.

Training the Toddler to Self-Feed

The freedom that comes with a toddler unit who can feed himself using a fork or a spoon is a great relief for many toddler owners. By the age of 2, many toddlers can effectively operate a spoon with a 75 to 80 percent efficiency, but most will not achieve complete mastery until age 3 or 4. Begin your toddler's training with a spoon, then use the same process to introduce a fork. Use the following strategy when introducing utensils to a toddler.

⚠ *CAUTION: Toddlers do not need to use knives. Owners should prepare their foods in proper portions and sizes.*

[1] When your toddler is 12 months old, purchase several different spoons. Allow your toddler to pick his favorite spoon and use it at mealtimes.

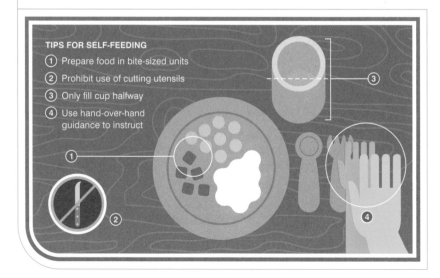

TIPS FOR SELF-FEEDING
(1) Prepare food in bite-sized units
(2) Prohibit use of cutting utensils
(3) Only fill cup halfway
(4) Use hand-over-hand guidance to instruct

[2] Use hand-over-hand guidance and modeling to instruct your toddler in proper utensil usage and etiquette.

[3] Provide positive reinforcement when your toddler effectively spoons food into his mouth.

EXPERT TIP: Many toddlers will alternate between the spoon and their fingers until they can master the utensil. Give your toddler the freedom to explore (and make a mess) when training. Initially, do not provide negative feedback to interfere with a toddler's utensil training.

Transitioning from a Sippy Cup to a Standard Cup

Most toddlers are eager to begin drinking from a regular cup by age 3 or 4.

[1] Take the lid off the familiar sippy cup.

[2] Pour a small amount of juice or milk into the cup. Never fill the cup more than half full until your toddler masters use of the standard glass.

[3] Guide your toddler. Place your hand over his hand as he grips the cup and show him how to slowly tip the container up to meet his lips, and then set the cup back down.

CAUTION: Do not use breakable cups or glasses when training the toddler.

Programming Mealtime Behavior Protocols

Mealtimes can be a challenge for toddler owners. Training a younger toddler how to operate the tools at her disposal may prove to be as difficult as keeping an older toddler interested in staying at the table. Overall, when programming your toddler's mealtime protocols, set reasonable goals and remain consistent with routines and limits.

[1] Divide responsibilities. Parent responsibilities include selecting and purchasing food, preparing meals, regulating the timing of meals and snacks, restricting food as necessary, attending to appropriate mealtime behavior, and providing consequences for inappropriate mealtime behavior. Toddler responsibilities include deciding how much (if anything) to eat.

[2] Set a good example by modeling good table manners and making healthy food choices. Prompt and practice important skills (e.g., saying "please" or "excuse me"). Teaching your toddler appropriate mealtime behavior is a long-term process—the correct behaviors must be repeated over and over before your toddler will demonstrate them on her own.

[3] Provide frequent praise ("You sat like a big girl at the table today") and brief physical rewards (e.g., hugs, kisses, love pats) for appropriate table behavior. Do not reward with food, especially candy or dessert, as this can make your toddler think of these foods as sources of comfort and love, making them more appealing than they already are.

[4] Ignore minor misbehavior (e.g., whining, food refusals, minor tantrums) at the table. Briefly turn away for 5 seconds without speaking to

or making eye contact with your toddler; then immediately return your attention when the toddler is behaving appropriately.

[5] Use a brief time-out (see page 161) for major misbehavior and rule breaking (e.g., banging utensils, throwing food, or purposefully dumping a plate). Time-outs at the table can be enforced by having all adults and siblings turn away briefly, by pulling the toddler's chair away from the table, or by turning the child's chair to face away from the table for a short time.

If you must use more than three time-outs in one meal, remove any remaining food items and end the meal. By ending the meal early, you avoid turning mealtime into a battle and creating negative associations with food. Experiencing a little hunger before the next meal or snack is harmless and may even motivate your toddler to behave herself at the next mealtime.

[6] Do not scold your toddler if she chooses not to eat; however, expect her to remain at the table for a reasonable length of time—about 10 minutes.

Reprogramming Picky Eater Models

Some toddlers are reluctant to practice change and variety when fueling. Use the following procedure to counter their tactics.

[1] Prepare your toddler's favorite foods occasionally and include at least one preferred food at each meal, but don't cave in to your toddler's requests to prepare only his favorite foods. Making your toddler's favorite meal every time will reinforce picky eating habits and can lead to avoidance of entire food groups. Respond to "I hate this" by saying, "Oh well, that's what we are having tonight," and then find another topic of conversation.

[2] Include your toddler when shopping for groceries, and allow him to safely take part in preparing meals. Creative, cooperative food preparation can help a toddler accept new foods. Cut foods into the toddler's favorite shapes or help your toddler use a cookie cutter to stamp out a sandwich in the shape of his favorite animated character.

[3] Keep a positive emotional atmosphere at the dinner table at all times. Avoid discussions about your toddler's eating habits. Don't provide increased attention during food refusal, whining, pleading, or tantrums.

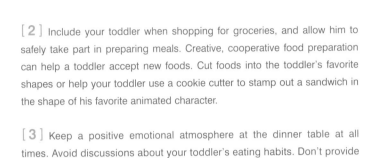 **EXPERT TIP:** *Many owners will cook one meal for the family and another for the toddler, assuming that the toddler will not eat what is prepared for the family. This strategy may develop your toddler into a picky eater. Offering the toddler the same food that you are eating will give him the opportunity to try new foods and develop healthier eating habits.*

[4] Praise each small step your toddler takes toward expanding his food choices. Show excitement when your toddler eats a small portion rather than urging him to eat more.

[5] Schedule mealtimes and snacks, and eat in the same location every day. Do not allow your toddler to eat between meals and snacks. Your toddler needs to experience hunger to appreciate the value of eating good food. Maintain about 2 hours between each meal or snack and offer only water to drink 1 hour before meals.

[6] Don't plead, bargain, coax, nag, or threaten your toddler about food during or between meals. Do not force-feed.

[7] Give independent toddlers some control by offering a choice between two reasonable, healthy food options ("Do you want an apple or yogurt?").

⚠ **EXPERT TIP:** *If your toddler refuses to eat from a range of food groups, ask your service provider if a multivitamin should be considered.*

Reprogramming No-Eater Models

If your toddler is showing standard energy levels and is growing normally, she is probably eating enough. If mealtimes are a struggle and your toddler appears to be eating very little, follow the tips above for "Reprogramming Picky Eater Models" in addition to those presented below.

[1] End each meal on a positive note even if your toddler refused to eat anything. Do not insist that the toddler drain the bottle, empty the cup, or clean the plate. Wait until the next meal to feed her, and do not allow her to eat once she leaves the table.

[2] Keep portion sizes small to allow your toddler to feel proud of her eating accomplishment.

⚠ **EXPERT TIP:** *Do not evaluate your toddler's caloric/nutritional intake on a meal-by-meal basis. If you are concerned, track your child's nutritional intake for an entire week and discuss the results with your toddler's service provider.*

[3] Provide frequent praise to the toddler for eating, trying new foods, using tableware appropriately, sitting, and using good manners.

PROTOCOL RECOMMENDATIONS

1. Mealtime duration: 10 minutes
2. Use time-outs to stop bad behavior
3. Do not force-feed or micromanage
4. Do not reward picky eating (or food refusal) by offering sweets or other desired food

MEALTIME BEHAVIOR PROTOCOLS: Program your model

by setting reasonable goals and remain consistent with routines and limits.

[4] Place your toddler in a brief time-out (see page 161) for whining, throwing tantrums, or repeatedly asking for snacks between meals.

EXPERT TIP: *Do not worry excessively about "food jags." It is not unusual for toddlers to accept only one type of food for a week and then refuse that same food the next week. Nutritional intake rarely suffers and these stages typically are short-lived.*

Reprogramming Sugar-Craving Models

Toddlers are preprogrammed to crave sweets, so owners must set limits and teach healthy food choices early on. Here are some suggestions to keep your toddler from eating too many sweets.

EXPERT TIP: *There are many misconceptions about the ill effects of feeding toddlers sugar. Sugar does not cause hyperactivity and does not directly cause diabetes (although being overweight increases the risk of developing it). The only proven harm of consuming too much sugar is increased tooth decay.*

[1] Limit the number and the type of sweets that you keep in the home, but don't place a complete ban on sugar. Eliminating sweets entirely may only propel your toddler to seek out more sugar.

[2] Make healthy choices while shopping for food. Consider keeping only a single flavor of ice cream in the freezer and one or two types of cookies.

[3] Gradually replace sugar-packed foods with healthier alternatives, including fresh or dried fruits, yogurt, graham crackers, and oatmeal cookies.

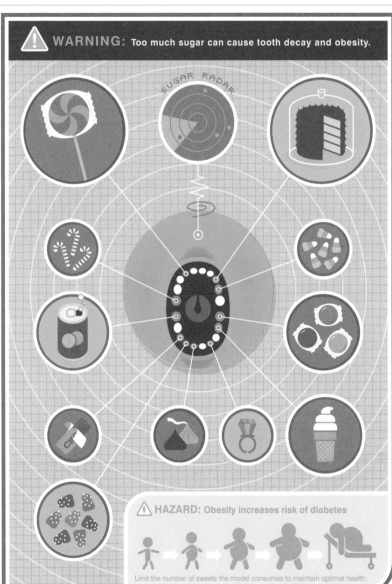

⚠ **EXPERT TIP:** *Avoid the dessert power struggle by including a single serving of dessert at the toddler's place setting along with the entire meal, thus giving it no special significance as a "treat." Even if your toddler eats dessert first, she will eventually learn to eat other dinner offerings to avoid becoming hungry before the next scheduled snack time.*

[4] Don't put sweet liquids in a toddler's bottle.

[5] Offer the toddler a wide range of nutritious foods, and restrict highly concentrated sweets to certain times or occasions. Don't give concentrated sweets (such as candy bars) for snacks.

[6] Don't use sugar-rich foods to bribe, reward, or quiet your toddler. Your toddler will come to associate these foods with feelings of love and comfort and will only desire them more.

[7] Place your toddler in a brief time-out (see page 161) for whining, throwing tantrums, or repeatedly requesting sugary candies or snacks.

Eating Malfunctions

Consult with your toddler's service provider if you notice any of the following eating malfunctions:

■ Your toddler is losing weight or has not gained weight in a six-month period.
■ Your toddler is gagging, choking, vomiting, or has difficulty chewing or swallowing foods.
■ Your toddler is frequently sick with upper-respiratory infections and/or aspiration-related illnesses.

- Your toddler develops a fever, vomiting, wheezing, hives, or diarrhea after eating specific foods.
- Your toddler shows pain or discomfort during or after meals.
- Your toddler eats a very narrow range of foods over a long time or is still refusing solids.
- Your toddler shows fear or anger or consistently cries at mealtime.

Chapter 4

Programming Sleep Mode

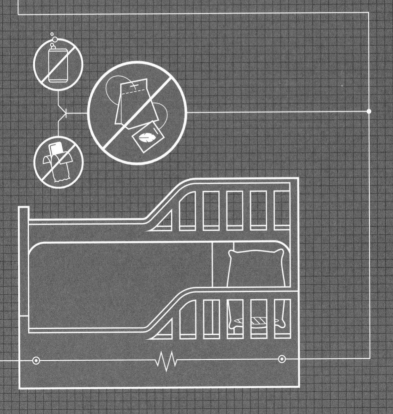

Configuring the Toddler's Sleeping Space

The toddler should be accustomed to falling asleep in the location that he is expected to remain in for the night. An ideal sleep environment is:

■ *Quiet.* White noise, such as air circulating through an electric fan, can be used to mask other noises that may otherwise activate your toddler.

■ *Dark.* A dim night-light can be used, but excessive light may delay sleep.

■ *A comfortable temperature.* Cooler temperatures (68°F, 20°C) promote better sleep.

■ *Safe.* Any perceived threat of danger will impair sleep.

Transferring the Toddler from a Crib to a Bed

The transition from crib to toddler bed (see page 18) usually is made in response to the impending arrival of a second unit or when a toddler can climb out of a crib on his own. Most toddlers make this transition between 18 and 40 months after installation.

When making this transition, choose a time that is relatively stress free, rather than a time filled with pressure (for example, the night before you bring home his new sibling). Transfer the toddler's favorite transitional objects (see page 84) from the crib to the new bed. Install a side rail to prevent damage from occurring if your model falls out of the bed, or place a thick quilt on the floor to soften the landing area until he learns his new sleeping boundaries.

Option One: Take down the crib and replace it with the new bed (placed in the same location). Slightly delay your toddler's normal bedtime on the first night to ensure sleepiness, and begin the "excuse me" method for teaching the toddler to self-activate sleep mode (see page 86).

Option Two: Install the new bed but leave the crib in place. Help the toddler become more comfortable lying awake in the new bed. Use it for calm activities like reading or storytime prior to bedtime. Later you can ask him if he wants to sleep in the new bed during naptime (or at nighttime if he is eager). Some toddlers will go back and forth between the crib and bed for a short while, but most will quickly settle into their new bed. Once the toddler is regularly sleeping in the bed, uninstall the crib.

Sharing Your Bed with the Toddler

Research indicates no long-term positive or negative outcomes from either bed sharing or solitary sleeping arrangements. Bed sharing does not cause problems when it is practiced on a regular basis (as opposed to reacting to a sleep problem), all night (as opposed to part of the night), and when parents discuss the issue and agree on bed sharing as a lifestyle choice (as opposed to moment-by-moment disagreements leading to inconsistent responses).

Review the advantages and disadvantages listed below and make the lifestyle choice that is best for your toddler and your family.

Potential Advantages

■ In various forms, bed sharing has been practiced throughout most of history and is still the normative practice in most societies.

■ It prevents excessive bedtime struggles and extended night waking.

■ It promotes easier and more convenient breast-feeding, which allows the female toddler user more sleep.

■ Some experts believe it promotes parent-toddler attachment and fosters a toddler's emotional development.

Potential Disadvantages

■ It may impede spontaneous sexual relations and negatively affect the marital relationship.

■ Because toddlers who bed share are more dependent upon parental presence to fall asleep, they are more likely to experience sleep problems when they must sleep independently.

■ Rollover accidents involving toddlers are rare, but still possible. A toddler sleeping on the edge of the bed can be knocked off the bed, get wedged between the bed and the wall, or bump her head on a nightstand.

■ Toddlers are active sleepers and move about during the night. These frequent movements may briefly wake parents many times per night.

■ Some experts say the practice impedes the development of autonomy, independence, and self-soothing.

■ For some toddlers, co-sleeping is a difficult practice to stop once it is an established habit.

⚠ *CAUTION: Do not co-sleep on a couch or waterbed, and never allow a toddler to co-sleep with an adult who is intoxicated.*

Understanding Upgrades in Sleep Mode

Through the toddler's development, total sleep duration per 24 hours will decline, primarily due to the reduction in daytime sleep from 1 to 5 years of age. Sleep ability, sleep timing, and sleep duration vary slightly

from model to model and should not affect overall functioning. Don't be alarmed by these slight variations; they are not manufacturer defects.

Your toddler's sleep schedule program is affected not only by internal settings, but also by the users' daily activity patterns and preferences, and therefore is adaptable to reprogramming and change.

Your unit must have sufficient sleep to function optimally during the day. If she displays any of the following features, your model may be impaired by insufficient sleep.

- Falls asleep quickly once restrained in a car seat
- Sleeps 30 minutes longer than usual if you don't wake her
- Becomes cranky, irritable, or has frequent temper tantrums
- Becomes overactive and distractible at certain times during the day
- "Crashes" very early at night after several days of insufficient sleep
- Sleeps an hour more or less than the daily norms for age (see chart below)

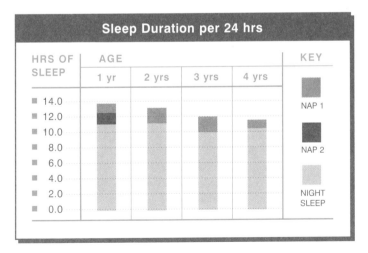

Sleep Duration per 24 hrs

HRS OF SLEEP	AGE				KEY
	1 yr	2 yrs	3 yrs	4 yrs	NAP 1
■ 14.0					
■ 12.0					NAP 2
■ 10.0					
■ 8.0					
■ 6.0					
■ 4.0					NIGHT SLEEP
■ 2.0					
■ 0.0					

Napping

Naps are short periods of time when the toddler enters sleep mode during the late morning or afternoon hours. Toddlers who take naps are more alert, attentive, and adaptable than those who do not. Most models require fewer naps as they upgrade.

12 to 20 Months

Most units are preprogrammed to skip the morning nap and slightly lengthen their afternoon nap at around 16 to 20 months following delivery. Structure and effective limit setting by parents become more important as the toddler leaves his crib and increases locomotion. Imagination and separation anxiety also peak, which may lead to sleep-related fears.

21 to 30 Months

By 21 months following delivery, 88 percent of models take only one daily nap. Your unit's increasing independence and quest for autonomy may lead to napping resistance, but do not respond by removing naps from your toddler's sleep schedule entirely, as your toddler will become overtired and therefore irritable, fussy, or even aggressive later in the day.

3 to 4 Years

The large majority of 3-year-old models still nap six days a week, but napping begins to drop off during the fourth year. Models in the final stages of the napping upgrade may not enter sleep mode during their scheduled nap time early in the afternoon. Nonetheless, schedule a time each day when you turn off the television, unplug the phone, and dim the lights. Your toddler will fall asleep occasionally, especially when most needed. Bedtimes may need to be a bit more flexible, adjusting slightly each night depending on whether the toddler slept during her daily nap opportunity.

Upgrading Sleep Mode to Self-Activate

By programming skills one step at a time, you will help your toddler self-activate important sleep habits while minimizing distress. Discuss the plan with all toddler users in the home before implementing; then begin when your toddler is healthy and showing no signs of illness or discomfort. Here are some general guidelines for reprogramming.

[1] Help your toddler become accustomed to and comfortable with falling asleep in the place where you want him to sleep the entire night. If your toddler has been falling asleep next to you in your bed, insist that he fall asleep in his own bed while you lie beside him until he is comfortable in the new environment.

⚠ **EXPERT TIP:** *The toddler's bed should not be associated with punishment or pain. Use another location for time-outs, and administer any painful medical procedures elsewhere.*

[2] Gradually modify the sleep environment to be compatible with sleep. A progressive method makes for a smoother transition as you upgrade your toddler's sleep program. For example:

■ If your toddler is uncomfortable in a dark room, reduce the overall light over a period of days by replacing a 60-watt lightbulb with a 40-watt, 20-watt, and finally a 7-watt bulb.

■ If the toddler is accustomed to watching television while falling asleep, begin by adjusting the volume lower and lower, then change the channel to a program that is uninteresting for the toddler, and finally turn off the television.

[3] Program a bedtime routine. Bedtime routines may include activities such as washing the face, brushing the teeth, changing into pajamas, and going to the bathroom. The routine should end with a positive, soothing activity (e.g., a story, a back rub, cuddling) that takes place in the toddler's bedroom. Other aspects of the routine may include:

■ Transitional objects. A favorite doll, blanket, or stuffed animal can help toddlers transition into restful sleep. Do not allow other toys in bed.

■ Light snacks and drinks. However, bottles in bed, excessive fluids, and heavy, late meals may disturb sleep. Avoid drinks or foods containing stimulants (cola, tea, chocolate) several hours before bedtime.

[4] Install the self-activating sleep mode program (see page 85). Nighttime awakenings are part of the preprogrammed sleep cycle in all toddlers. Those models who are programmed for independent sleep initiation will quietly reactivate sleep on their own, but models who are programmed to activate sleep while being held, rocked, sung to, or fed will awaken during the night and use their audio system to retrieve a parent to help them to reinitiate their sleep program.

[5] Maintain a very strict sleep schedule until the upgrade is complete and your toddler sleeps well for two weeks. Once this milestone is achieved, you can initiate some flexibility with timing. However, the better you can keep your toddler on a predictable schedule, the more your toddler will adapt by sleeping when you want him to be sleeping. A consistent morning wake time across schooldays, weekends, and holidays will produce the best results.

[6] Reward your toddler for even small steps toward success. This can be accomplished through the use of a sticker chart, a small prize from a

grab bag, or social reinforcement (e.g., hugs, kisses, reporting success to friends/relatives when your toddler is present).

[7] If your toddler is resisting every step of the way and you are making little progress, help your toddler reprogram skills during the day. If the toddler is highly oppositional at bedtime, teach him to follow instructions and accept consequences during the day (see page 176). If your toddler shows separation anxiety during the night, help him develop independent play skills (see page 142) and to handle separation during the day (see page 138).

Installing the Self-Activating Sleep Mode Program

Here are several methods for teaching your toddler to fall asleep without your presence. As long as you consistently promote your toddler's independent sleep initiation and self-soothing programs, your toddler will soon be able to self-activate sleep mode. Use sleep strategies to first target bedtime, then night wakings, and finally naps.

EXPERT TIP: If your toddler shares the room with a sibling, the sibling may need to temporarily sleep in another location until your toddler unit is fully programmed for sleep.

Ignoring with Parental Presence

The advantage of this approach is that it reduces child distress compared to simply leaving the room and letting the toddler cry. The disadvantage is that you may have to repeat this procedure several times a night until your toddler becomes confident falling asleep without your presence.

[1] Lie down on a mat or cot in the toddler's bedroom, but act like you are sleeping and do not interact with your toddler. The goal is to reduce your toddler's reliance on your actions and words to help him fall asleep.

[2] Ignore crying, protests, and special requests until the toddler falls asleep; then sneak out of the room.

The Walking Chair

[1] Sit in a chair, reading a book until your toddler falls asleep.

[2] Over successive nights, gradually move the chair farther and farther away from his bed. Your toddler may protest when you are no longer in direct line of sight, but if you continue with the program your toddler will adapt.

The "Excuse Me" Drill

[1] Delay the toddler's bedtime by 15 to 30 minutes the first night.

[2] Sit next to your toddler on his bed, stroking his head and back. Say to the toddler, "Excuse me, but I need to go check on the dog (or another reasonable excuse). I'll be right back."

[3] Leave the room, quickly returning after just a few seconds to praise the toddler for remaining quietly in bed.

[4] Continue to regularly walk in and out of the toddler's bedroom to provide attention, physical presence, calm touch, and verbal praise whenever the toddler is quiet, lying down in bed, and calm.

[5] Gradually delay your visits from every few seconds to a maximum of every 15 minutes. Make sure you leave the room while the toddler is still awake so he learns to fall asleep without parental presence. If the toddler behaves inappropriately (e.g., screams, cries out), remain out of the room until the child is lying in bed calmly and is quiet.

[6] Once your toddler falls asleep quickly (15 to 20 minutes) and independently, slowly fade the bedtime earlier over the next few nights until you reach your toddler's original bedtime.

Unmodified Ignoring

This reprogramming approach works quickly—most toddler models respond by the third night, especially if you temporarily delay his bedtime slightly to make sure he is sleepy. However, many toddler owners experience distress during this procedure because of the audio cues the toddler transmits to show his unhappiness.

[1] Place your toddler in bed, give him his final hug and kiss, turn off the lights, and walk out the door.

[2] Ignore the toddler's cries or calling out. Do not return unless absolutely necessary (e.g., if illness or danger is suspected).

⚠ *EXPERT TIP: It is purely a myth that crying will harm your toddler. Research has found no detrimental effects of cry-it-out approaches to sleep. In fact, studies found only positive effects on toddler sleep, mood, adjustment, and family functioning.*

Suppressing Premature Exits from the Bedroom

[1] Enter the toddler's bedroom occasionally when he is lying quietly in bed to reinforce the positive behavior.

[2] If your toddler leaves the room, immediately escort him back to bed while remaining calm and quiet. Do not yell at or spank the toddler, as this will only heighten his level of stimulation and make it more difficult for him to fall asleep. Repeat this procedure as many times as necessary, or until you are so exasperated that you need to progress to the next step.

⚠ **EXPERT TIP:** *For older toddlers, reprogramming may be easier if you allow the toddler some amount of control. Laminate an index card or give him an expired credit card as a "bedroom pass," which he can exchange for one short permitted trip out of his bedroom.*

[3] Some stubborn models require a physical barrier to keep them in their bedrooms at night until the activation of the program upgrade is complete. Place a baby gate in the doorway of the room, or close the door and secure it with a plastic doorknob safety cover or a hook-and-eye latch. Close the gate or door quickly in response to misbehavior; then immediately open it again once your toddler self-calms and decides to remain in his bedroom. *Do not leave a bedroom door secured all night.*

Reprogramming Sleep Mode for Travel

Toddlers often do not adapt well to changes in their sleep environment. Vacations can be especially difficult due to changes in settings, unusual sleeping arrangements, and alterations of their sleep schedule.

Some models' sleep programs are easily adaptable; these toddlers should pose few problems during the trip. In these cases, allow yourself to be more flexible and respond to your toddler's sleepy signals rather than setting a strict schedule. Other models may not adapt to the changes of environment so easily; in this case, the toddler owner must plan, prepare, and schedule for best results.

[1] Book a hotel or cabin that allows for sleep arrangements similar to those in your toddler's usual environment (e.g., separate bedroom or sleeping area, or a king-sized bed if you plan to bed share). If necessary, use blankets or furniture to construct barriers between the toddler's sleep space and other living areas.

[2] If you foresee any difficult changes, practice before your trip. For example, have the toddler practice sleeping with a sibling in the same bed if this will be the arrangement during the trip, or put the toddler to sleep in a portable traveling crib for a few naps and then take the crib with you on the trip.

[3] Take along the toddler's familiar bedding items and sleep aids (pillow, blanket, stuffed animal, pacifier, fan or other white noise machine).

[4] Adhere to your toddler's normal sleep schedule as closely as possible. Otherwise, your toddler will become overtired and cranky and become even more difficult to get to sleep.

EXPERT TIP: *A sedating antihistamine can be used as a last resort in activating the toddler's sleep mode while traveling. However, some models react adversely to antihistamines and become even more agitated.*

[5] Remain flexible about temporarily bending some of the normal sleep rules.

[6] Immediately return to your toddler's normal schedule and sleeping arrangements when you return home. Don't keep any part of your vacation sleeping mode for even a night, as this will confuse your toddler and make for a longer readjustment period.

Sleeping Malfunctions

Although the most difficult parts of upgrading the toddler's sleep mode involve activation and maintenance, some models will experience occasional processing malfunctions. These malfunctions may occur abruptly during sleep mode, causing heightened concern and anxiety among owners. The following trouble-shooting guidelines should help users correctly diagnose and repair unsettling nocturnal malfunctions.

Nightmares

Nightmares are frightening dreams that awaken the toddler from sleep. Toddlers with frequent nightmares do not necessarily have emotional problems. Stressful experiences and adjustment periods, such as starting preschool, initiating self–waste disposal, or adjusting to the delivery of another unit, can trigger nightmares, as can normal toddler fears and anxieties. Other triggers can include illness, fever, and starting or stopping certain medications.

Toddlers who have an occasional nightmare only will need comforting and reassurance. If your toddler is having frequent nightmares, the following approaches may be helpful.

[1] Make sure your toddler is getting sufficient sleep and has a regular sleep schedule.

[2] Physically comfort the toddler upon her awakening from a nightmare. Reassure her by saying, "It was just a dream." Listen as the toddler attempts to verbally express the frightening dream content. Remain calm and reassuring, but avoid excessive attention, lengthy discussions, or psychoanalyzing.

[3] Differentiate dreams from reality by pointing out strange or unbelievable aspects of the dream. For example, say, "You must have had a bad dream because you know that dogs don't talk in real life." Do not play along with your toddler by pretending to combat make-believe monsters or initiating monster-proofing rituals.

[4] Once the toddler has calmed down, return your model to her own bed to sleep. Bringing the toddler into your bed may speed her return to sleep that night, but this practice could encourage your toddler to report nightmares during normal nighttime awakenings to receive your special attention.

[5] Identify and eliminate experiences that may be overwhelming for your toddler. Maintain consistent daily routines so that separations and pickups are predictable. Eliminate scary movies and television shows. Do not allow your toddler to witness or overhear discussions about family stresses such as marital conflict or money or work problems.

[6] Use daytime exercises to help your toddler confront and master her fears. Identify a common theme or feared object in your toddler's nightmares. For example, nightmares about separation may be addressed by arranging brief and predictable separations from a parent.

POSSIBLE TRIGGERS:

1. Starting preschool
2. Self-waste disposal
3. Adjusting to the delivery of another unit
4. Starting or stopping certain medications
5. Illness or fever

NIGHTMARES: Stressful experiences, adjustment periods, or regular anxieties can trigger this sleeping malfunction.

Sleep Terrors

Sleep terrors often begin with a sudden shriek or scream. The toddler may appear frightened, agitated, and confused. She may be unresponsive or reject your attempts to calm her, and may stare blankly through you with glassy eyes. These terrors occur when the toddler's sleep program gets stuck between stages of deep sleep and wakefulness. This program glitch may occur about the same time every night, about two to three hours after falling asleep. Glitches are more likely to occur among toddlers who are excessively sleepy from staying up late, waking early, or giving up their daily nap. Illness, fever, certain medications, and environmental noise may also trigger program glitches. Toddlers who snore or have difficulty breathing due to sleep apnea, congestion, or allergies (see page 206) are also more likely to display sleep terrors.

[1] Increase the toddler's sleep time by ensuring a regular schedule, addressing bedtime dawdling and nighttime awakening, or reinstating naps.

[2] Introduce an electric fan or other white noise to mask environmental noises that might trigger a program glitch.

[3] Avoid awakening or restraining the toddler during a sleep terror, as this may escalate her behavior. Gently help her back to sleep.

[4] Try scheduled awakenings. Gently awaken the toddler about 15 to 30 minutes before the expected sleep terror by placing your hand on her shoulder and shaking gently until her eyes open or she emits a mumble, then allow her to fall back to sleep. If the toddler arouses easily, awaken her 15 minutes later the next night. If the awakening triggers a program glitch, awaken her 15 minutes earlier the next night.

[5] Perform these scheduled awakenings nightly until your toddler achieves seven consecutive nights without a glitch. Next, eliminate one night each week until the awakenings are no longer necessary. If the toddler experiences another event, add another night of awakening. Continue until your toddler's sleep-wake programming is running smoothly.

Night Playing

Most models programmed for self-activation of sleep mode (see page 85) who awaken at night will quickly return to sleep. However, some models will awaken in the middle of the night and appear happy, alert, and ready to play. If this describes your toddler, the following suggestions may help.

[1] In many cases of night playing, the toddler is no longer tired because she is getting sufficient sleep at other times. Reduce her time in bed to more accurately reflect her sleep needs. First, copy and complete the sleep chart in the appendix (see page 216) and add up your toddler's total daily sleep time, including naps. Use this number (e.g., 12 hours) to schedule her allowable time in bed (e.g., 9 hours at night and 3 hours during the day). Do not allow sleep outside of scheduled times, even after extended nighttime awakenings. This plan may make your toddler tired and irritable at first, but she will be noticeably less interested in nighttime play by the third or fourth night.

[2] Eliminate toddler access to rewarding and stimulating activities at night. Keep the television turned off, the lights dimmed, and your interactions boring and neutral so your toddler does not think it is time to play.

Chapter 5

General Maintenance and Training

Waste Disposal

Until your toddler is trained for self–waste disposal (see page 99), and during her initial training, you must continue to change the toddler's soiled diapers and/or underwear. Though many users find this process tedious, the benefits far outweigh the inconvenience.

When away from the home, the continued use of the diaper bag is recommended. Adapt supplies to your toddler's growing needs—larger diapers, training pants, a change of underwear or two, and so forth. Your toddler's new cognitive abilities may also require the addition of more complex toys or simple board books that she can use to entertain herself during changing sessions.

Diaper Change Upgrades

The new mobility that a toddler acquires will require an updated set of changing procedures. If you find that your unit dislikes lying down for a diaper change, you may want to use an upright changing method. Use this method only after the toddler is capable of balancing on one leg (when holding onto a support).

[1] Place your supplies within reach of the changing area.

[2] Kneel in front of your toddler with the toddler facing you.

[3] Direct the toddler to pull her pants down, or pull them down for her. Remove any soiled diapers or undergarments to avoid greater mess. Instruct the toddler to hold your shoulder or another nearby support. Set aside any soiled garments.

[4] Clean the toddler as necessary. You may find it easier in a standing position to lean (or ask the toddler to lean) slightly forward when cleaning the area.

[5] Instruct the toddler to stand with her feet about shoulder width apart to replace a diaper, or replace the soiled underpants with a clean pair if your toddler is training for self–waste disposal. Replace the top layer of clothing.

Programming the Toddler for Self–Waste Disposal

Programming a toddler for self–waste disposal, or "toilet training," can be one of the most difficult challenges toddlers and toddler owners face. For toddlers, learning to use the toilet independently means mastering a complex chain of skills. Some toddlers eagerly embrace the opportunity and practically train themselves, while others may fight the process. It is important that the toddler owner stay relaxed, no matter how the toddler reacts.

Signs That Your Toddler Is Ready (Fig. A)

Before you start the training process, make sure your model is prepared for success. Most typically developing, healthy toddlers are ready to begin training by around 24 to 30 months following delivery. Girls tend to be ready earlier than boys. Your toddler should exhibit the following behavior before you install the self–waste disposal program upgrade.

■ Motor skills. Your toddler should be able to pick up objects, lower and raise her pants, and walk from room to room easily.

■ Bladder and bowel maturity. Your toddler should be staying dry for a few hours at a time, urinating only 4 to 6 times a day, and fully emptying the bladder. If your toddler frequently wets small amounts (7 to 10 times a day), you should wait to train. If your toddler has a recent history of constipation (hard stools, painful bowel movements) or tries to avoid passing bowel movements, talk with your toddler's service provider.

■ Receptive language. Your toddler should be able to understand toilet-related words like "pee," "poop," "wet," "dry," "clean," "messy," and "potty."

■ Willing and able. Your toddler should be able to imitate simple tasks (e.g., clapping hands). She should understand and be willing to follow simple instructions, such as "come here, please" or "sit down." If your toddler opposes you much of the time or has frequent temper tantrums, work on this behavior before toilet training (see page 169).

■ Bladder and bowel awareness. Your toddler should be able to indicate that she is aware of the need to urinate or defecate. Many toddlers show awareness by making a face, assuming a special posture like squatting, or going to a favorite location when they urinate or defecate. They may also tell you when they are about to go or have just finished going.

⚠ *EXPERT TIP: Do not allow yourself to be pressured by others into toilet training if the time is not right for your family. Pick a time when the household is reasonably stable and will continue to be so for a few weeks. Do not begin toilet training if you just moved or plan to move soon, if you are expecting or just had a new baby, or if you have experienced a recent illness, death, divorce, or other family crisis. If you have already started toilet training, however, and your toddler continues to make even slow progress during these times, you don't need to place her back in diapers. Continue, but be patient.*

Preparation for Reprogramming

[1] Model correct toileting behavior. Let your toddler come with you into the bathroom and explain what you are doing ("Mommy is going pee-pee in the potty"). Male owners should model by sitting on the toilet until the toddler is fully reprogrammed for self–waste disposal.

[2] Teach your toddler to raise and lower her pants (see page 113).

[3] Teach your child to follow your instructions (see page 176).

[4] Purchase a potty chair and encourage your toddler to sit on it. Several weeks before you start toilet training, place a potty chair in the bathroom. Help your toddler decorate the chair with stickers or write her name on it. Encourage your toddler to sit on it while fully clothed. Introduce calm activities like looking at a book or playing a game while your toddler sits on the chair. Never force your toddler to sit on the chair against her will. Shortly after your toddler begins sitting on the potty chair, parents can start transferring solid waste from the diaper into the toddler's potty chair as she watches.

⚠ *CAUTION: Some potty chairs come equipped with a splash guard that could hurt your toddler as he tries to seat himself and make him reluctant to use the chair. If you prefer a potty chair with a splash guard, make sure that it is made of soft, flexible plastic or that it is removable, just in case.*

[5] Praise your toddler every time she does any part of toileting behavior correctly ("You did a great job pulling down your pants"). Smile and provide hugs and kisses. You may also add stickers, stamps, or other small tangible rewards for success.

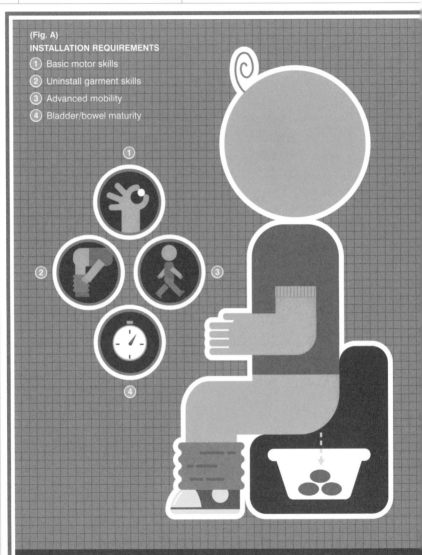

(Fig. A)
INSTALLATION REQUIREMENTS
1. Basic motor skills
2. Uninstall garment skills
3. Advanced mobility
4. Bladder/bowel maturity

SELF—WASTE DISPOSAL: This essential program can be installed

(Fig. B)
PROGRAM LAUNCH

by utilizing the Gradual Method or through Concentrated Training Sessions.

Reprogramming: The Gradual Method

[1] Pick a convenient start date, and completely stop using disposable diapers except during sleep times. Modern disposable diapers are constructed so well that they wick away moisture, reducing toddler discomfort following accidents. They also seal very well, so they delay owner's detection of toileting accidents (and therefore prolong the self–waste disposal reprogramming process).

⚠ *CAUTION: Placing your toddler in a diaper when accidents are "inconvenient" will confuse him and extend the reprogramming process.*

[2] Prompt your toddler to sit on the potty chair. More frequent sits of shorter duration are better than fewer sits of longer duration. Start with very brief sits (5 seconds) and slowly work up to around 3 minutes each. You can occasionally extend a sit to 5 minutes if you think production is near. Schedule sits during times that your toddler is most likely to produce waste, such as 15 to 20 minutes after a meal or waking from a nap.

💡 *EXPERT TIP: Male toddlers should be encouraged to always sit on the potty chair (instead of standing to urinate) until they are fully trained for both urine and bowel disposal. Female toddlers need to be taught to wipe from front to back to avoid infection.*

[3] Reward your toddler for correctly eliminating waste and provide encouragement and praise for any correct part of appropriate toileting. For many toddlers, simple praise will be sufficient. Others may require the addition of tangible rewards like stickers, stamps, or candies. Some toddlers love to flush the toilet, so reserve this "privilege" for when they produce.

[4] Expect accidental releases. Maintain your sense of humor and plan for accidents. Keep a bag with extra sets of underwear, clothing, and wipes with you at all times. Don't criticize, scold, lecture, or punish. Remain neutral yet encouraging ("I bet you'll get your potty in the potty chair next time"). Do not leave your toddler in wet or dirty pants—you want to instill the feeling of being clean and dry.

Reprogramming: Concentrated Training Sessions

While very few toddlers complete toilet training in one day, parents can speed the process by launching with a concentrated training session. Choose a convenient start date, such as a day when you will be at home and free from distractions like work, chores, and visitors. Do not try to get anything else accomplished except teaching your toddler toileting skills.

All the basic components of the previous method still apply, but you will add the steps listed below during sessions. You may choose to schedule several two-hour "concentrated" training sessions per week during the early stages of training, backing off as your toddler masters the skills. If your toddler reacts negatively to these concentrated sessions, discontinue them for a couple weeks and follow the gradual program.

[1] Increase your toddler's fluid intake. Increasing the amount your toddler drinks will provide more frequent opportunities for him to learn to use the toilet. About an hour before a session, begin to gently encourage your toddler to drink at least 8 ounces (237 ml) of liquid per hour. Offer a variety of beverages.

[2] Provide your toddler with frequent prompts to sit on the potty. Give a reminder at least every 15 minutes during the sessions. Watch your toddler closely for physical cues or mannerisms (facial expressions, grabbing,

crossing legs, squatting, squirming, passing gas) that suggest your toddler is ready to expel waste. Quickly take his hand and walk to the potty chair for a sit.

[3] Check for dry pants every 5 minutes. Use a timer to remind yourself to check your toddler's pants to see if they are still dry. Praise ("Good boy, your pants are dry") or provide small rewards for dry pants during concentrated sessions.

[4] Use "practice runs" to the potty chair immediately following every accidental release. When you find that your child has wet pants, say matter-of-factly, "You wet your pants, so let's practice going to the bathroom." Quickly change the wet pants for dry ones; then take your toddler to the scene of the wetting accident or where your child was when you discovered the wet pants. Calmly lead your toddler to the bathroom. Help him lower his pants, sit down on the toilet (for a second or two), stand up, and pull the pants up. Return to the place where the accident occurred. Repeat this procedure until your toddler has made five practice trips.

⚠ **EXPERT TIP:** *Postpone toilet training for a few weeks if your toddler isn't making progress or you find yourself getting upset about it. Consider contacting your child's physician if your toddler:*
- *refuses to sit on the potty or toilet*
- *reacts negatively anytime the topic of toilet training is mentioned*
- *is constipated or withholding bowel movements*
- *is older than 4 years and not yet toilet trained during the day*

Nighttime Training

Nighttime bladder control may lag daytime control by months or, in some cases, years. At 2 to 3 years following delivery, only 45 percent of female models and 35 percent of male models remain dry throughout the night. It is normal for most units to occasionally wet the bed until they are 5 or 6 years old.

Once your toddler is fully reprogrammed for self–waste disposal during the day, use the toileting diary on page 214 to track the number of times he wakes up dry. If he is wet nearly every morning upon awakening, then keep the diaper or training pants for a while. If he is dry more nights than wet, he is developing bladder maturity. Consider removing the diaper and protecting the mattress pad with a waterproof mattress cover. Using two layers of bedding (sheet, mattress cover, sheet, mattress cover) will allow you to strip one layer in the middle of the night if your toddler experiences an accident. Eliminating the diaper will provide the "bladder-ready" toddler necessary feedback (wetness, discomfort) to teach him to control his bladder and wake to use the bathroom.

Avoid large amounts of fluid and caffeine before bedtime, but do not restrict fluids altogether. Praise and/or rewards should be provided for dry nights. Punishment is never recommended to discourage bed-wetting.

Public Restrooms

Always accompany your toddler into public restrooms. Children under 4 years old can join you in the restroom corresponding with your gender, regardless of their own. A 3-year-old toddler may balk at walking into the "wrong" bathroom but will usually do so with an owner who insists.

Training the Toddler for Self-Cleaning

Continue to clean your toddler to guarantee optimal functioning of the unit. Although you don't necessarily need to bathe your unit daily (in fact, daily bathing may add to some toddler skin conditions [see page 204]), many models enjoy the ritual of the bath at night before bedtime. Continue to bathe your toddler as you did when she was a baby, and use the techniques below to update your toddler's self-cleaning programming.

 CAUTION: *Never leave your toddler unattended in the bathtub!*

Self-Washing

When teaching your toddler to wash herself, allow your toddler to explore with a washcloth and soap. The more comfortable she is with these tools, the more likely she is to use them properly.

You may want to get in the tub with the toddler to demonstrate how to wash properly. Wet the cloth, apply some soap, and let the toddler do the scrubbing.

Hair Washing

When teaching your toddler to wash her own hair, use the following technique.

[1] Get in the bath with the toddler.

[2] Hand the toddler a cup and let her fill it with water.

PROGRAMMING SELF-CLEANING MODE

PROGRAMMING TIPS

1 Demo mode will trigger download mode

2 Always supervise the bathing process

3 Overbathing can cause dry skin

[**3**] Direct the toddler to pour the water over your head. This will be fun for the toddler, and she may want to repeat this action many times.

[**4**] Direct the toddler to pour the water over her own head. You may need to build up to this, as many toddlers are reluctant to immerse their heads in water. If this is the case, allow the toddler to wet her head with a wash cloth or by leaning back (with your support) and dipping her hair in the water.

[**5**] Apply, or let your toddler apply, a small amount of baby-safe shampoo to her head. Scrub the shampoo into lather.

[**6**] Direct the toddler to close her eyes and repeat step 4. Clear any remaining shampoo from the toddler's face before directing her to open her eyes.

EXPERT TIP: *Allow your toddler to wash your hair so that she can see the process that is taking place. Her familiarity will expedite her self-cleaning programming.*

Hand Washing

Teach your toddler to wash her hands frequently before she reaches her second birthday. Wash your hands together with the toddler to program this function. Set the water to a cooler temperature, and do not allow your toddler to move the hot-water faucet handle. Initially, hold your toddler's hands under the running water, apply soap to the fronts and backs of her hands, scrub, rinse, and dry.

When programming self–hand washing, direct the toddler to perform one of these actions and then help her with the remaining ones. Once she masters holding her hands under the water, direct her to perform the soap application procedure and then help her with the rest. Repeat this process until your toddler has mastered all hand-washing functions.

Dental Care

It is not necessary to take your toddler to the dentist until he is 2 years old, unless he has experienced dental trauma (see page 203). However, early dental hygiene programming will set your toddler up for a lifetime of healthy teeth. Many units will not brush their own teeth effectively until they are 4 or 5 years old. In the meantime, you should allow your toddler to become comfortable with and experiment with his toothbrush. Show him how you brush your own teeth, and direct him to mirror the same movements with his own.

If your toddler enjoys brushing his own teeth, inspect his teeth when he is done and finish the job. Remain positive as you search for "shiny" spots. You or your toddler should brush his teeth at least twice a day. Additionally, brush your toddler's tongue to care for halitosis.

Many toddlers dislike the taste of toothpaste. You may elect to brush your toddler's teeth with only water on the brush, or secure a training toothpaste (with an attractive, toddler-friendly tube and that is safe to swallow) and use it sparingly.

EXPERT TIP: Use dental paraphernalia that features his favorite animated characters to inspire interest in a reluctant toddler. Or secure several different toothbrushes and allow your toddler to choose which one he would like to use each time he brushes his teeth.

Training the Toddler for Self-Dressing

The continued use of clothing is recommended for all toddler units. By the time your toddler is 2 years old, she may be able to remove one or two loose items of clothing. Many toddlers will not develop the physical skills to put these clothes back on without help until they are 3 to 3 1/2 years old, whereas the mental desire to dress on schedule may not develop for several years more. Help your toddler practice self-dressing, but do not push these skills on an unwilling unit.

EXPERT TIP: As your toddler's interest in self-dressing grows, her interest in what she wears will increase. If you are uncomfortable allowing your unit to wear whatever she chooses, offer her two choices of clothing. Many toddlers in search of independence will appreciate the "control" they are offered when given a choice, and you can be sure that the choice she makes from those you've offered will be appropriate for the weather and occasion.

Select clothes that meet the following standards to ease the self-dressing process:

■ Loose-fitting shirts with wide neck openings.

■ Loose-fitting pants with elastic waistbands.

■ Few—if any—buttons, snaps, or zippers. Ties present a strangling hazard and should be avoided, especially around the neck.

■ Slip-on shoes or shoes with Velcro strapping.

EXPERT TIP: Owners can allocate their assistance in accordance with their toddler's ability by using a technique called scaffolding*. Help your toddler with the parts that she really needs help with, and then fade out your* *assistance as the toddler develops her own skills. For example, open a pant leg wide to allow toddler foot entry, and then back off as the toddler pulls the pants up around her waist. Praise your toddler for completing the act.*

Underwear and Pants Installation

[1] Ask your toddler to lie down on his back (Fig. A). You may lie on your back as well to teach by example.

[2] Raise your legs and your toddler's legs straight up in the air so they form a 90-degree angle with the ground (Fig. B).

[3] Show and tell your toddler how to insert each of his feet into the appropriate holes of the underwear (Fig. C). You may have to perform this step for your toddler until his coordination feature has fully developed.

[4] Instruct your toddler to grasp the elastic waistband of the underwear and pull them toward his waist (Fig. D). Show him how to shimmy the underwear down and over his hips.

[5] Set your toddler's feet flat on the ground with his knees bent. Instruct him to raise his butt off the ground by pressing down on his feet and up from his hips.

[6] Advise the unit to continue pulling the underwear into place. Once complete, placement should be checked and adjusted, and praise should be given.

[7] Repeat with the toddler's pants (Fig. E).

(Fig. A)
BASE MODEL

(Fig. B)
LAY FLAT ON BACK WITH LEGS IN AIR

(Fig. C)
INSERT LEGS THROUGH HOLES

(Fig. D)
INSTALLATION COMPLETE

(Fig. E)
REPEAT B–D TO INSTALL PANTS

SELF-DRESSING: Training the model to install his own clothing can be

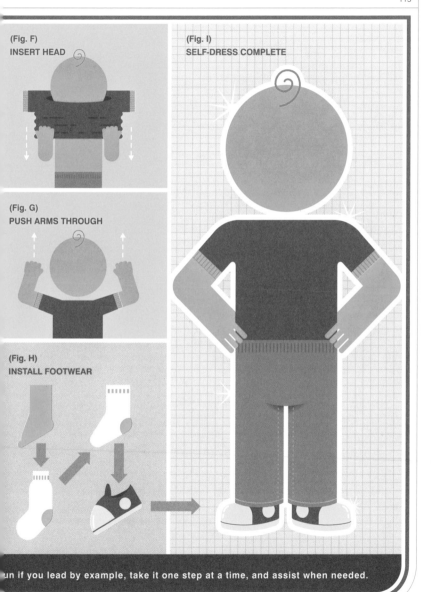

(Fig. F)
INSERT HEAD

(Fig. G)
PUSH ARMS THROUGH

(Fig. H)
INSTALL FOOTWEAR

(Fig. I)
SELF-DRESS COMPLETE

...un if you lead by example, take it one step at a time, and assist when needed.

⚠ **EXPERT TIP:** *If your toddler has access to an older unit, have the younger toddler observe the older child as he dresses himself. The modeling may teach your toddler to dress himself more quickly.*

Shirt Installation

Provide your toddler with a loose-fitting, wide-neck, short-sleeved shirt for practicing shirt installation. Remain patient; this process can be frustrating for a toddler to learn.

[1] Bunch a T-shirt up from the base to the neck, and instruct your toddler to grasp the shirt at the back of the neck.

[2] Help the toddler insert her head into the neck opening (Fig. F). Gauge your toddler's level of patience. If she is enjoying the process, allow her to have fun. If she is becoming frustrated, increase your level of hands-on help and instruction.

[3] Instruct your unit to grasp the bottom of the shirt and pull her head all the way through the opening.

[4] Hold the base of the shirt for your toddler and help her to insert her arms into the openings (Fig. G). Assist her only as much as necessary until both arms are inside the sleeves.

[5] Check and adjust the shirt if necessary.

⚠ **EXPERT TIP:** *Encourage your toddler to dress a doll or stuffed animal to practice zipping, buttoning, snapping, and installing clothes.*

Sock and Shoe Installation (Fig. H)

The installation of socks and shoes requires advanced programming and may be too complex for a young toddler model. Allow your toddler to explore sock and shoe removal (both hers and yours) to help her understand how these items fit on the feet.

[1] Stretch a sock over your toddler's toes. It is recommended that parents perform this step in the early stages of self-dressing, as this can be a difficult maneuver.

[2] Have the toddler sit down and grasp the top of the sock on both sides.

[3] Point your toes and ask the toddler to do the same.

[4] Show and tell the toddler how to pull the sock up until her toes touch the tip. You may need to assist the toddler in getting the sock over her heel.

[5] Repeat steps 1 through 4 for the other foot.

[6] Open a shoe as wide as it can go. Unbuckle any buckles, open any Velcro clasps, or untie and loosen any laces.

[7] Place the tip of one of your toddler's feet into the shoe. You should hold the tongue (if any) of the shoe up out of the way.

[8] Instruct the toddler to hold your shoulders as she stands up into the shoe. Show and tell her how to clear her heel past the back of the shoe (if any).

[9] Repeat steps 6 through 8 for the other foot.

⚠ **EXPERT TIP:** *Consider practicing shoe installation with a backless shoe or sandal to help ease the process. Though these may at first prove difficult to walk in, your toddler will soon get the hang of it. Initially, your toddler may be more adept at taking shoes off than putting them on. Encourage both activities.*

Jacket Installation

When programming the toddler for self-jacket installation, use the following procedure.

[1] Lay the jacket (front side up) on the floor. Open the front of the jacket and lay the arms out to either side. Be sure that the arm holes are exposed and accessible.

[2] Direct the toddler to stand at the top (neck side) of the jacket, but not on top of it.

[3] Direct the toddler to insert each of his arms into the arm hole openings. He will have to bend slightly and you will likely have to help him insert his arms into the holes. Be sure that each arm is about halfway down each jacket sleeve before proceeding to step 4.

[4] Direct the toddler to keep his arms in the sleeves and raise them up over his head. You may have to assist him if the garment gets caught on his head.

[5] Fasten the jacket, or direct your toddler to do so.

Dealing with a Slow- or No-Dressing Model

Many toddlers will not dress themselves when prompted, even though they are capable of doing so. Confirm that your toddler has the motor skills necessary to dress himself before proceeding with the following strategy.

[1] Tell the toddler that he has a set time limit in which to get dressed (10 to 20 minutes), and set a kitchen timer for the appropriate amount of time.

EXPERT TIP: Praise your toddler frequently when establishing and teaching dressing skills. Begin by praising every minor accomplishment—putting an arm through a shirtsleeve, for example—whether the task is done perfectly or not. Focus on praise until your toddler gets the hang of dressing, then correct backward shirts or pants or a shoe on the wrong foot.

[2] Check on your toddler every few minutes in the early stages of training, but allow your toddler some independence with his time.

[3] If your toddler dresses before the timer goes off, praise his accomplishment and offer him a reward, such as 10 to 20 minutes of your time, a sticker, or another small prize. If your toddler does not dress himself before the timer goes off, direct him to continue dressing himself. If necessary, after 5 to 10 minutes, complete the dressing for him. Do not play games or discuss any topic other than dressing while doing so. Do not reward the toddler.

ANGRY
ANT
APPLE
ARM
ASK
AXE
BABY
BACK

(A) Audio Input
(V) Video Input
(A/O) Audio Output

Chapter 6

Growth and Development

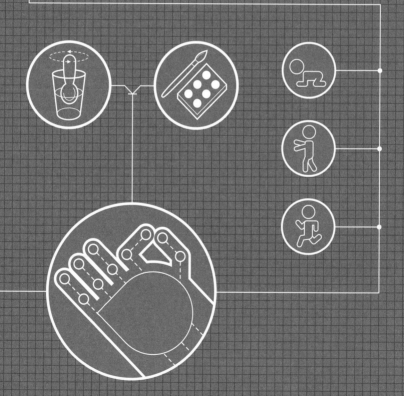

Physical Growth and Development

The rate at which toddler models increase in both height and weight is considerably less than the rate at which your unit grew during the first year after delivery. Between the ages of 12 and 24 months, the average toddler model adds 5 inches (13 cm) and 4 to 5 pounds (1.8–2.3 kg). From 24 to 36 months following delivery, standard models gain another 2 to 3 inches (5–8 cm) and an additional 5 pounds (2.3 kg).

Monitoring the toddler's physical development is aided by calculating her percentile. This number describes how your toddler is growing in relation to national averages of the same age and sex. Weight and height are most often considered when determining the percentile, and sometimes head circumference is also considered.

To determine your toddler's percentile, measure her height and weight and write down the numbers. Then use the graphs on pages 123–124 to find your toddler's percentile. On the graph appropriate to the gender of your unit, find your toddler's age along the bottom, and your toddler's height (in inches or centimeters) and weight (in pounds or kilograms) along the side. Draw a point where your toddler's age intersects with her height and weight.

If your toddler is in the 20th percentile for weight, for example, she weighs more than 20 percent of other toddlers in the country. Note that many models are in different percentiles for different measurements.

Do not place too much concern on your toddler's percentile. A toddler in the 10th percentile for height can grow up to be quite tall. The most important factors in determining a toddler's growth pattern are the growth patterns of her parents. People who were small during infancy may have similarly small children.

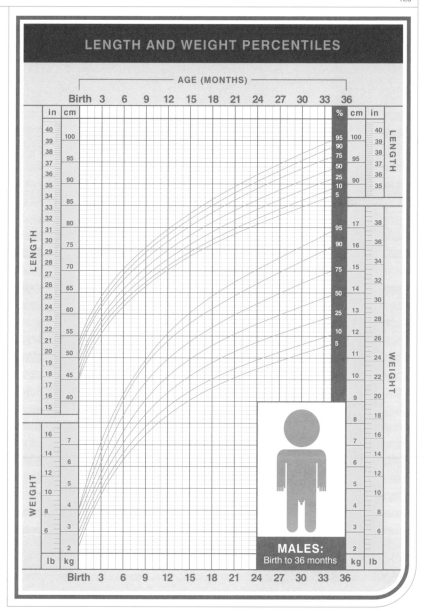

LENGTH AND WEIGHT PERCENTILES

MALES:
Birth to 36 months

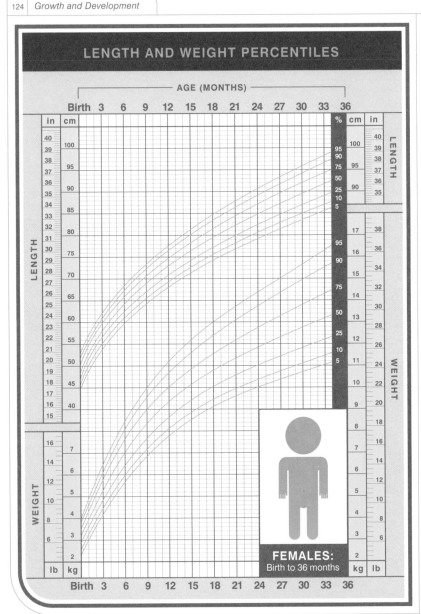

LENGTH AND WEIGHT PERCENTILES

FEMALES: Birth to 36 months

*⚠ **EXPERT TIP:** Multiply a boy's height at age three by 1.87, and a girl's height at age three by 1.73, to determine your toddler's approximate adult height.*

Dental

Your toddler unit will continue to produce teeth in her mouth. These will grow until the toddler is around 3 years old and then will eventually fall out and be replaced by permanent adult teeth (beginning between 6 and 7 years old). A full set of toddler teeth includes:

- Four second molars
- Four first molars
- Four canine teeth
- Four lateral incisors
- Four central incisors

These teeth will appear in a variable order from model to model; however, standard arrival of toddler teeth generally follows a set course:

- Central incisors between 6 and 16 months
- Lateral incisors between 9 and 16 months
- Canines between 16 and 23 months
- First molars between 13 and 19 months
- Second molars between 20 and 33 months

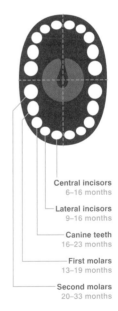

Central incisors
6–16 months

Lateral incisors
9–16 months

Canine teeth
16–23 months

First molars
13–19 months

Second molars
20–33 months

Do not be concerned if your model does not follow this schedule exactly. As long as your toddler has a mouthful of 20 teeth by the time she is about 3, she is within acceptable specifications for dental development. Continue to care for your toddler's teeth and train her to do so on her own (see page 111).

Movement and Mobility

Typical models will have begun to crawl and pull themselves up on furniture or sturdy objects by the time they reach toddlerhood, but it is during the toddler years that your unit will truly develop increased mobility. Standard models "cruise," or walk while holding onto furniture or other objects, at around 12 months after delivery and typically follow with a first unsupported step shortly thereafter. By around 15 to 18 months, most toddler models are able to carry things while they walk, though their movements are still fairly uncontrolled. Between the ages of 18 and 24 months, most models begin to move more quickly, though most still lack the balance and control necessary to handle short stops and starts. After 24 months, most toddlers develop more control and coordination, learning such skills as jumping and climbing stairs one foot at a time (versus crawling or climbing up stairs). By 36 months, your unit will move with confidence and assurance, exhibiting skills such as skipping, standing on one foot, stopping with precision, throwing a ball accurately, and changing directions without losing balance.

Physical Milestones

As your toddler matures, he will begin to meet various physical milestones—but since every model is different, not every toddler will reach a specific milestone at a given time.

The physical milestones described on the following pages are based on the average among different models. Do not be alarmed if the toddler you received does not match these set averages. There is always a range of performance, and deviations from average do not reflect favorably or unfavorably on the toddler's abilities. If you have genuine concerns about your toddler's development, contact your toddler's service provider.

12 to 18 months

Between 12 and 18 months following delivery, most toddler models:

■ Slow in their growth pace. Your toddler may have tripled his birth weight in the first 12 months after delivery, but now growth begins to decelerate (see pages 123–124 for averages).

■ Pull themselves to a standing position to "cruise" furniture by 13 months, and walk independently by 14 months. *Note:* Toddlers with larger heads and larger bodies tend to walk a bit later, because more muscle development is required to function efficiently.

■ Use their thumb and index finger to grasp small items.

■ Explore objects less by mouth and more through visual and tactile means.

■ Are "into everything." Your toddler's increased mobility leads to more exploration, experimentation, and mastery of the physical environment. Safety is a serious matter at this age—a toddler-proof environment and owner vigilance are required for optimum function (see page 180).

■ Repeatedly practice new skills like stacking, climbing, and manipulating.

■ Use hand gestures, like pointing with an index finger, to signify when they want something.

■ Can scribble with crayons or markers.

■ Can throw, toss, and roll a ball.

■ Can stir with a spoon.

18 to 24 months

Between 18 and 24 months following delivery, most toddler models:

■ Learn to stand on one foot.

■ Use tools (a play hammer), utensils (spoons), or crayons.

■ Start to develop a hand preference for some activities, but this may change from day to day.

■ Walk more effortlessly.

■ Run and climb onto furniture, on top of cabinets, up the stairs, and out of the crib.

■ Are astute observers and imitators of others' actions.

■ Can kick a ball forward.

24 to 30 months

Between 24 and 30 months following delivery, most toddler models:

■ Can stack, organize, and pile similar toys.

■ May be able to catch a large ball thrown from a short distance.

■ Master the ability to run, hop, skip, and jump.

■ Can almost fully dress themselves and are highly adept at undressing themselves.

■ Can balance on one foot briefly.

■ Can ride a wheeled toy on the floor with alternating feet.

30 to 36 months

Between 30 and 36 months following delivery, most toddler models:

■ Have developed a hand preference for most activities.

■ Can catch large balls.

■ Have developed foot coordination to jump, kick a ball, pedal a tricycle, and walk up and down stairs using alternating feet.

■ May begin to trace or copy basic shapes with a crayon.

■ Can work a simple puzzle.

Verbal Development

Some models may begin to make sounds that resemble words in your language as early as the age of 6 months. Throughout the toddler years, most models' language programming upgrades to include actual words, phrases, and sentences, and eventually nonstop paragraphs. Most units begin to speak between the ages of 10 and 18 months, but the rate at which the upgrade occurs varies widely from model to model. Typically, a 12-month-old toddler knows around 6 words, a 24-month-old toddler may know as many as 400 words, and a 36-month-old toddler can express thousands of ideas in complete sentences.

Here are some techniques you can use to encourage your toddler's language program upgrade.

[1] Talk to your toddler. The more your toddler hears the words you use, the more familiar they will become, and the more likely he will be to use them too.

[2] Name objects and things. Point to a cat and say "cat." Point to a chair and say "chair." Eventually, your toddler will repeat the names back to you,

increasing his vocabulary and familiarity with common words. When he is older, he will begin to ask you for the names of various objects.

[3] Narrate your activities. Describe your actions in detail so your toddler hears words in their proper context. Say, "First, I'm going to help you take off your shirt, and then I'm going to change your diaper. Here are the diaper wipes so that I can clean you up."

[4] Expand on the words your toddler emits. If your toddler says "truck," respond by saying, "Yes, there is a red truck pulling into the gas station." The positive response lets your toddler know that he named the object correctly, while the expanded sentence provides more words in their correct context, helping your toddler to make sense of his observation.

[5] Keep your sentences short and simple so your toddler can follow along. Once he's developed more language skills, you can increase the complexity of your speech patterns and vocabulary.

[6] Read books. Hearing stories read aloud exposes your toddler to the connection between words and meaning in addition to a broader vocabulary.

[7] Play games. Point to an object and ask your toddler to name it. Ask things like "What does a cow say?" to help him increase his cognitive abilities.

Verbal Milestones

12 to 18 months

Between 12 and 18 months following delivery, most toddler models:

■ Respond to their own name.

■ Begin to imitate or use a few simple words to communicate. First words usually involve a familiar person or object (bottle, mama, ball).

■ Master the meaning of the word "no."

■ Combine words with gestures.

■ Can say anywhere from 2 to 50 words.

■ May recognize 3 to 100 words, many more than they can speak.

■ Can understand simple directions like "Please get your coat."

18 to 24 months

Between 18 and 24 months following delivery, most toddler models:

■ Use words for people, animals, toys, food, and other familiar nouns, along with some simple verbs (go, run).

■ Can say from 10 to 100 words.

■ Can understand up to 400 words.

■ Will frequently use the words "me," "mine," and "no."

■ Use one- to two-word utterances ("all done," "uh-oh").

■ Go through the "naming explosion," during which the toddler may triple his vocabulary in a matter of weeks by constantly asking a toddler owner "What's that?"

24 to 30 months

Between 18 and 24 months following delivery, most toddler models:

■ Begin to put together two-word sentences.

■ Add verbs, pronouns, and adjectives to their vocabulary.

■ Master the names of body parts, shapes, and colors.

■ Continue using largely self-focused language, with words like "I," "me," "mine," and "no."

■ May talk out loud to describe their own ongoing behavior.

30 to 36 months

Between 30 and 36 months following delivery, most toddler models:

■ May understand over 1,000 words.

■ Make rapid gains in learning the rules of grammar and syntax.

■ May still make logical speech errors (e.g., "goed there," "my foots").

■ Improve word pronunciation.

■ Increase sentence complexity.

■ May begin to relate long stories or experiences.

■ Seek to understand the world by frequently asking for an explanation of specific events ("Why?").

Emotional and Social Development

Your toddler is full of uninhibited emotions between the ages of 12 and 36 months. He is mastering many new physical, cognitive, and verbal skills, and he craves independence. At the same time, however, the quest to learn all of these new things can be overwhelming. He is not yet able to express himself verbally and is physically not yet capable of being as self-sufficient as he'd like to be. This contradiction leads to temper tantrums and emotional meltdowns.

Your toddler may also be exposed to new social situations during this time in his life. He may meet his first friends and experience new playthings and situations. At first, your toddler will not be skilled at sharing or taking turns with a playmate, but with proper training and as his emotional and social skills develop, by the time he is 3 years old he will begin to show signs of socially acceptable programming.

Toddler temperament and parenting style set the stage for social development. Toddler owners need to support the toddler's curiosity and exploration without becoming overcontrolling or confrontational, yet balance this with supervision and flexible limits to ensure safety. For guidelines on programming your toddler's social and emotional development, see Chapter 7: Discipline.

Emotional and Social Milestones
12 to 18 months

Between 12 and 18 months following delivery, most toddler models:

- Develop an intense interest in exploring and mastering the physical environment. Successful explorations can lead to increased autonomy, independence, and feelings of self-worth.
- Use nonverbal signals to communicate (hold arms in air to be picked up; point with index finger to desired objects).
- Mimic the actions of others.
- Show affection.
- Begin to pretend play, usually imitating a familiar activity with props, such as drinking from a cup.
- Display a rudimentary recognition of social cues by providing appropriate responses to facial expression, vocal tone, and volume.
- Play independently and parallel (alongside) same-age peers.
- May bite and hit peers to assert self and protect territory or toys.
- Feel an ambivalent desire for closeness to yet independence from toddler owners.

18 to 24 months

Between 18 and 24 months following delivery, most toddler models:

■ Display a significant push toward independence by wanting to do everything "myself."

■ Show increased irritability, negativity, temper tantrums, defiance, and oppositional behavior. The infamous "terrible twos" actually peak about this time, before the second birthday.

■ Play alongside peers (parallel), with little turn taking or interaction.

■ Show more complexity in their pretend play, including dressing up or practicing familiar routines like feeding or bathing a doll.

■ Feel concerned for and try to comfort someone who is upset or crying.

■ Tend to get over being upset quickly without holding a grudge.

24 to 30 months

Between 24 and 30 months following delivery, most toddler models:

■ Continue to test limits and display their independence while closely observing their owners' reaction.

■ Participate in interactive games.

■ Begin to respond to societal demands for greater self-control (e.g., compliance, sharing, cooperative play with others).

■ Become increasingly skilled at reading social cues (facial, vocal) to interpret others' feelings.

■ Fall into "mini-obsessions" about desired clothing, food, or activities. May show a desire to keep hands (or diaper) clean.

■ Thrive on (and may insist upon) consistent daily routines.

30 to 36 months

Between 30 and 36 months following delivery, most toddler models:

■ May begin to use simple planning strategies.

■ Exhibit rapid gains in self-help skills and social interaction.

■ May begin to show a preference and affection toward certain friends or playmates.

■ Begin to understand and internalize rules (but not the reasons).

■ May begin to apologize for misbehavior and recognize such in others.

■ Begin to identify with their own gender ("boy" or "girl") and to distinguish masculine and feminine sex-typed roles, games, and activities. Looks to use the appropriate public bathroom facilities.

■ Show an increased interest in humor and acting "silly" yet may not have a good sense of appropriate time and place.

■ May increase self-control, agreeableness, desire to please, and interest in peer relationships.

■ Integrate cooperative peers in pretend play to take on familiar roles ("I'll be the daddy, you be the mommy").

■ Enter the beginning stages of considering the thoughts, feelings, and wishes of other people, which helps with sharing and taking turns.

Training the Toddler for Care Outside the Home

Babysitters or day care centers can be used when neither toddler owner is available for supervision of the toddler. Some toddlers will adapt easily to new environments and caregivers, while others will exhibit signs of agitation and distress. Your toddler's reaction to separation will depend on his temperament, the presence of familiar people, his familiarity with the setting, and the physical characteristics and behavior of the stranger (e.g., how that person approaches and interacts with the toddler). In either case, a gradual transition is recommended.

TRAINING FOR CARE OUTSIDE THE HOME

TRAINING TIPS

1. Let him explore and interact with the new environment
2. Arrange play dates with other toddlers
3. Always say good-bye
4. Indicate the benefits of the new environment
5. Gradually increase time apart

[1] Slowly introduce your toddler to the new care situation. Spend time with your toddler in the new environment and with the new caregiver before leaving him there alone. This will help both you and your toddler to feel comfortable with the situation. Make several brief visits together before leaving your toddler at the new facility alone.

[2] Allow your toddler to explore his new environment and relate to his new caregiver. Let your toddler examine new toys or books or connect with his caregiver on his terms, in his own way. If the toddler shows reluctance, hold his hand or stay close to him as the two of you explore the new environment together. Tell your toddler's new caregiver about topics that interest your toddler to help them form a bond.

[3] Talk to your toddler about the upcoming change. Point out the positive things about the new environment, like the toys or the other children who also attend the facility.

[4] Arrange supervised "play dates" with a toddler who attends the day care center that your toddler will attend.

[5] Begin by separating from your toddler within the facility for short periods of time. Tell your toddler that you are going to the bathroom or going for a drink of water but that you will be right back. Say a simple good-bye, leave for several minutes, and then return. Allow the toddler to experience the separation. Next, begin to leave the facility for gradually longer periods of time. Leave with a smile, and never sneak out or leave without saying good-bye.

⚠ **CAUTION:** *Many toddlers will cry when left in others' care. This is a built-in program with many models. It may take your toddler one to three weeks before he is completely comfortable with his new environment.*

[6] Continue to lengthen your time away, working up to the full day. Say good-bye to your toddler, and stay away for an hour, half a day, and finally a full day. Seeing that you leave but always return as you promised will activate your toddler's trust.

[7] Show pleasure when you return to your toddler, but don't get over-emotional or he will conclude that the separation was difficult for you.

Overcoming Separation Anxiety

Toddlers who exhibit pronounced distress over separation from a parent are experiencing separation anxiety, a program malfunction that develops in many toddlers at between 18 and 24 months but can last much longer. Distress decreases as the toddler is programmed to activate self-calming, playing with others, and self-entertaining skills.

Your toddler's separation anxiety will be difficult for both of you at first, but your toddler's ability to reprogram himself to deal with the separation will closely reflect your behavior as you separate from him. Remain caring and empathetic ("I know it's hard to say good-bye"), but don't fall into the trap of providing excessive reassurance. Allow the toddler to experience minor distress, and over time he will reprogram himself. Face the change slowly to help a toddler grow accustomed to separation.

[1] Have your toddler leave the room without you. If your toddler is very clingy or tends to "shadow" you wherever you go, start with having the toddler leave you to "fetch" his favorite items or toys from a bedroom or playroom.

[2] Bring an unfamiliar caregiver into your home. Ask a babysitter to come to your home (unfamiliar person, familiar setting) while you shop for groceries or go out with a friend for an hour.

[3] Take your toddler to visit a familiar person in a less familiar setting. Drop your toddler off briefly with grandparents, friends, or relatives for an hour.

[4] Establish a separation routine. Predictable routines can help a toddler overcome anxiety about transitions. Likewise, separation routines will help your toddler adjust—inform the toddler when you will return, kiss him, hug him, wave to him, and go out the door.

EXPERT TIP: Longer-term problems with separation are often the result of learned behavior. When confronted with an impending separation, toddlers learn to behave in ways that encourage parents to remain longer, to return quickly, and to reduce the frequency of separation opportunities. Many times your best efforts to "help" your toddler—extra hugs, kisses, verbal reassurance—simply confirm to him that there is reason to be nervous. These efforts also reinforce problem behaviors and prevent toddlers from developing their own self-comforting/coping skills. Stick to your separation routine, keeping it brief and positive.

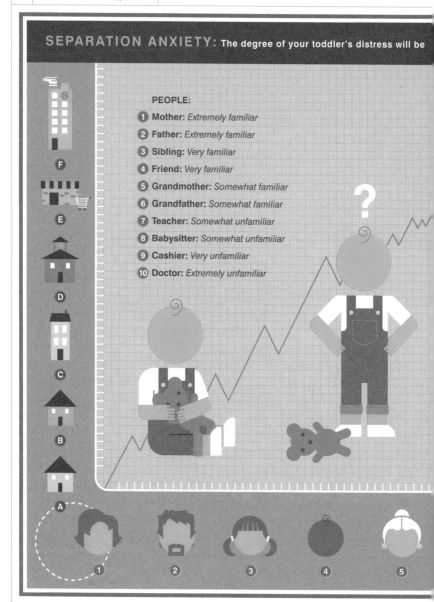

SEPARATION ANXIETY: The degree of your toddler's distress will be

PEOPLE:

1. **Mother:** *Extremely familiar*
2. **Father:** *Extremely familiar*
3. **Sibling:** *Very familiar*
4. **Friend:** *Very familiar*
5. **Grandmother:** *Somewhat familiar*
6. **Grandfather:** *Somewhat familiar*
7. **Teacher:** *Somewhat unfamiliar*
8. **Babysitter:** *Somewhat unfamiliar*
9. **Cashier:** *Very unfamiliar*
10. **Doctor:** *Extremely unfamiliar*

inversely proportional to his familiarity with the people and environment around him.

PLACES:

A **Home:** *Extremely familiar*

B **Relative's house:** *Very familiar*

C **Friend's house:** *Somewhat familiar*

D **School/Day care:** *Somewhat unfamiliar*

E **Supermarket:** *Very unfamiliar*

F **Doctor's office:** *Extremely unfamiliar*

6 7 8 9 10

Training the Toddler for Self-Entertaining

Training the toddler for self-entertainment develops an important skill that benefits both toddler and toddler owners. Toddlers who can play independently tend to be more resourceful and imaginative and to develop a greater sense of self-reliance. Unscheduled time and even occasional boredom will promote essential self-management skills that your toddler will soon need to behave successfully in social situations. Although temperaments and attention spans for self-entertaining vary greatly across individual models, all toddlers can be taught to self-entertain if the following skills are introduced gradually.

[1] Fill a couple of special activity boxes with toys that promote solitary play, such as those that involve constructing, creativity, or pretend play. Puzzles, shapes, blocks, crayons and paper, picture books, dolls, play houses, and adult-sized dress-up clothes (hats, shoes, purses, jewelry, or wallets and briefcases) are all good options. Rotate the boxes, or add and subtract toys to keep them fresh and interesting to the toddler.

[2] Shut off the television and go to a quiet room. Unveil the box of "fresh" toys and actively engage your toddler in play. Remain active and close to your toddler.

[3] After a few play sessions, become more passive in your participation. Play and talk less and simply watch the toddler play.

[4] Slowly edge farther away, eventually to a chair to read. The toddler may protest at first, but gradually persist as she becomes more and more

comfortable playing alone. Look up occasionally to describe and praise her behavior or go to her to provide positive physical attention.

[5] Over the next few play sessions, begin to excuse yourself briefly from the activity when the toddler is highly engrossed in play. Make up a reason, such as "I need to go check on something" or "I'll be right back." Come back after a few seconds to provide praise and physical touch for playing nicely. Gradually extend the duration of these "excuse me" periods to allow her to play by herself, but always return to provide positive attention in the form of praise and physical contact. Eventually, you will be able to come and go without your toddler noticing.

⚠ **CAUTION:** *Teaching your toddler self-entertainment does not mean you can be lax in supervising her.*

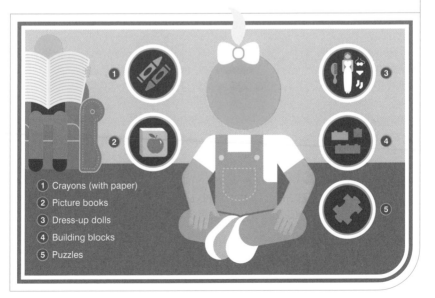

1. Crayons (with paper)
2. Picture books
3. Dress-up dolls
4. Building blocks
5. Puzzles

Removing Pacification Devices

Service providers are now less concerned about a toddler's attachment to transitional objects like blankets, pacifiers, and stuffed animals than they were 10 years ago. Habitual behaviors like thumb or finger sucking or strong attachment to objects are not generally harmful to the toddler, either physically or emotionally. However, if you are concerned about your toddler's use of the transitional object, here is a method for weaning your toddler.

[1] Begin by restricting use of the pacification device to certain locations, such as at home or in the car (the exception being an overnight stay). Do not allow the toddler to take the transitional object into public places.

[2] Next, restrict the pacification device for use during sleep times only (bedtime and nap time). Place it out of reach until the prebedtime winddown routine. For many toddlers, this may be as far as you wish to go in the removal process. There may be no reason to remove the pacification device from the toddler's private area (bedroom) and sleep time. Privatizing the pacification device removes the potential for social stigma (teasing) and reduces the duration and potential impact on the face/teeth (in the case of oral pacification devices).

[3] To completely remove the object, gradually begin to whittle away at the device to reduce the level of pleasure. Snip away at the blanket or progressively cut away at the tip of the pacifier (for one-piece models only). Your toddler will notice and protest, but she may just denounce the item as defective and throw it away herself.

Thumb and Finger Sucking

Thumb and finger sucking are considered separately because the toddler maintains owner's rights throughout, which makes breaking the habit a much more difficult task. Don't pressure your toddler to quit thumb sucking. Getting upset, nagging, or yanking her thumb out of her mouth will increase her desire to resist.

For young toddlers, the best approach is to ignore the behavior. Provide praise and reinforcement when she's not sucking her thumb, especially during circumstances when the behavior usually occurs. She may grow out of the habit herself.

For an older toddlers who is more motivated to stop, reminders such as private hand signals can be used to increase her awareness without alerting others. Similarly, a bandage on the thumb can serve as a helpful reminder. Objects to keep her hands busy or chewing gum to keep her mouth busy might help during high-risk times.

If more aggressive reminders are required, purchase commercially available bitter-tasting liquid. Use the fluid to coat the thumb or fingers when the toddler awakens in the morning, after each time that thumb sucking is observed, and again just before bedtime. Add a reward program for short periods of no thumb sucking (e.g., 3 to 4 times daily, especially during high-risk situations). This combination of fluid plus rewards has proven to be an effective strategy when used consistently.

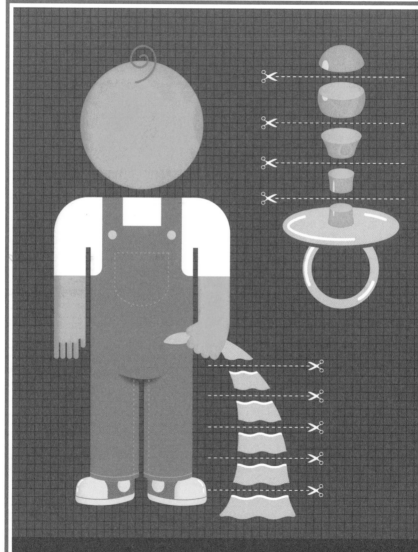

UNINSTALLING PACIFICATION DEVICES: Gradually snip

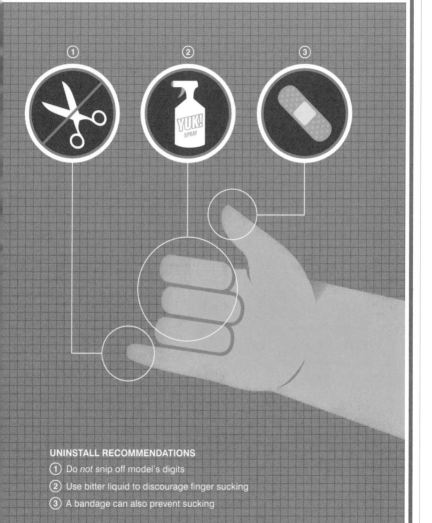

UNINSTALL RECOMMENDATIONS

① Do *not* snip off model's digits

② Use bitter liquid to discourage finger sucking

③ A bandage can also prevent sucking

away at pacifiers and blankets; appendages will require a different approach.

Preparing the Toddler for the Delivery of a Second Unit

The arrival of a second baby is a major adjustment for the whole family. Your toddler will probably display initial excitement over being a big brother or big sister to the new unit, but this behavior often wears off as soon as the toddler realizes that the new baby competes for toys and his parents' time and attention.

There are a number of factors that may influence how your toddler accepts the second unit, including his age (older toddlers tend to be more accepting), temperament (those with difficulty making transitions and intense reactions may display more problematic behavior), the quality of the relationship with his parents (a close relationship with the female owner may mean a more difficult adjustment), the presence of preexisting behavior problems, and each parent's own emotional state.

Typical positive reactions your toddler may show when introduced to the second unit include increased maturity and independence and increased caring and empathy for others. Short-term negative reactions may include increased expressions of anger/aggression/resentment, clingyness or separation anxiety (see page 138), and regressive behaviors involving sleep, waste disposal, and requests to be held or given a bottle. Fortunately, these behaviors usually decrease by the third or fourth month, and a difficult adjustment doesn't necessarily predict a poor sibling relationship later on.

The following suggestions will help promote a smooth adjustment as your toddler learns to interface with a second unit.

[1] Tell your toddler about the delivery of the new unit in advance. A good time to begin the preparation may be when the female user starts

showing signs of being pregnant, though others prefer to wait until the third trimester so the toddler doesn't have as long to wait before the baby is delivered. Teach the toddler basic information about babies and the birth process, and begin to prepare the toddler in many small doses over weeks.

[2] Include the toddler in planning for the second unit, such as picking out clothing, infant toys, and supplies, or decorating the nursery.

[3] Keep routines as regular as possible. Big changes, such as moving to a new home or a new preschool and transferring the toddler from the crib to a bed should be done well in advance of the second unit's arrival. If the toddler has not mastered self–waste disposal well before the unit arrives, delay implementing the self–waste disposal program until a new routine has been established after the additional unit's delivery.

[4] Male toddler owners should increase their involvement and role in caregiving (playing, dressing, feeding, bathing) for the toddler. This will limit the number of dramatic changes for the toddler and help minimize changes to the routine after the arrival of the second unit.

[5] Make advance arrangements for the child to stay with a family member or familiar person while the mother is in the delivery room. Arrange for phone calls and brief visitations to the hospital to see the mother and the second unit after it arrives.

[6] When the baby first arrives for home installation, the female user should try to focus her attention on the toddler while others hold the baby. Buy the toddler a small gift from the new unit, and include the toddler in pictures with the infant.

[7] Include the toddler in routine care of the new unit by asking him occasionally to retrieve diapers, bottles, and the like. Toddlers usually like to help and should be encouraged to do so. Don't overdo it or your toddler may resent the activities and, in turn, the new baby. Overachieving toddlers who want to help with everything can be encouraged to carry out caregiving activities with a favorite doll.

[8] Schedule regular times or special events for the older child during which he can have the parents' undivided attention. Newborn units typically sleep 16 hours each day, so spend some of this time playing with your toddler.

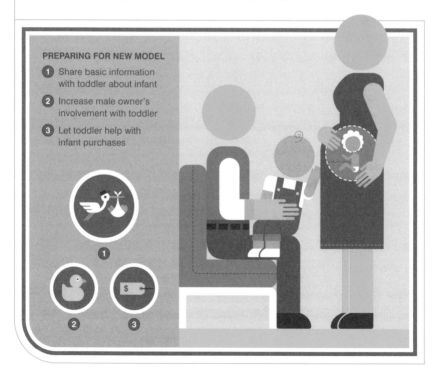

PREPARING FOR NEW MODEL

1. Share basic information with toddler about infant
2. Increase male owner's involvement with toddler
3. Let toddler help with infant purchases

[9] Rather than punishing or prohibiting regressive behavior, point out the toddler's special status as the older sibling and point out all the abilities and privileges that go along with being grown-up, such as eating ice pops and playing on the jungle gym.

[10] Establish some basic rules about handling the new unit. Examples may include requiring the toddler to ask permission before holding the newborn and before giving the baby a toy or food, and teaching him never to cover the baby's head.

[11] Praise the toddler for gentle, appropriate treatment of the baby.

[12] Respond immediately to any aggressive behavior your toddler displays toward the new baby. Although this aggressive behavior is not uncommon and may be purely unintentional (such an overzealous attempt to hug or kiss the baby), it is important to provide clear boundaries and deliver immediate consequences, such as a brief time-out (see page 161).

[13] Do not lower your expectations for appropriate behavior from your toddler. While you will be understanding during this difficult transition, do not tolerate outright misbehavior.

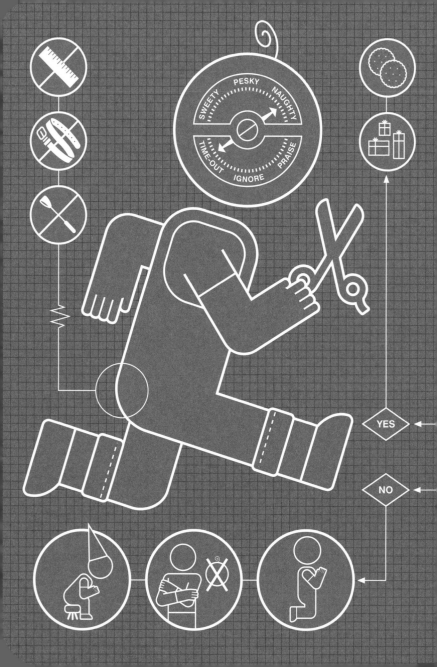

Chapter 7

Discipline

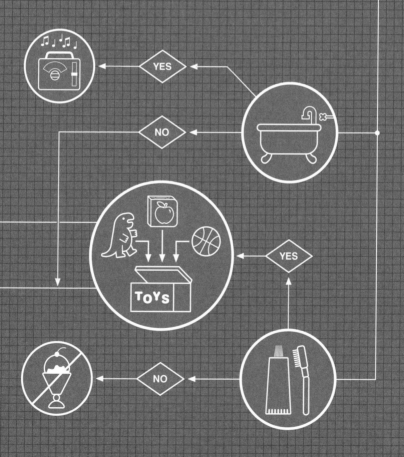

Upgrading
Toddler Behavior Protocols

For most toddler owners, the word "discipline" evokes images of using some form of punishment to decrease undesirable behavior. In truth, the term refers to a system of teaching, instruction, and behavioral program upgrading.

Because your toddler comes preprogrammed with a strong personal will, it is critical to pick your battles and remain firm yet positive. Firm parenting will teach your toddler to abide by societal rules and expectations. Positive reinforcement will help produce a well-functioning toddler who enjoys being around others. Learning appropriate behavior will lead to increased self-esteem and increased safety, and will prepare your toddler to learn and socialize.

Use the following general strategies to install upgraded toddler behavior programming.

■ *Establish routines.* Divide the day into morning, afternoon, and evening; then choose your activities within these blocks of time. Keep your toddler's sleep time and mealtimes consistent each day, so his internal clock can adjust to the routine.

■ *Identify a few reasonable goals, but also intersperse less-structured activities throughout the day*. Tasks and routines should be arranged from hardest to easiest, or least fun to most fun, to maintain your motivation leverage. For example, tell your toddler that you'll go outside to play on the swing after he puts his clothes in the laundry basket.

■ *Avoid placing unreasonable expectations on your toddler when he is sick, tired, hungry, bored, stressed, or in an unusual situation.*

■ *Anticipate potential problems.* Toddler-proofing your home (see page 180) will remove many of the more dangerous temptations for which you would need to be constantly scolding your toddler. Avoid situations that are sure to cause problems, like taking your toddler out to a restaurant for dinner before he's able to sit through a meal at home.

■ *Model appropriate behaviors yourself.* Actions speak louder than words. Your toddler comes equipped with a fully developed sensory system that picks up on and attempts to imitate the behaviors of others around him, especially the actions of his primary users. A parent can continually tell a child to get along with his sibling, but he will not follow these instructions if he is frequently exposed to bickering between his parents.

■ *Do not exhibit the very behaviors you are training against.* For example, do not yell at your toddler for yelling. Your toddler will be overwhelmed by your input and will not comprehend your message—in fact, you will actually be reinforcing the bad behavior.

■ *Be firm.* Toddlers need to learn to follow the rules and instructions set forth by authority figures. Providing your toddler with choices is a good strategy if there truly are alternatives, but sometimes an adult decision is required ("It's time to brush your teeth").

■ *Aim for immediate impact.* The duration of a consequence is not as important as the immediacy and the impact the action creates for your toddler. If you have the choice between removing one toy for three weeks (low impact, long duration) or removing access to all toys for 2 minutes, choose the latter. Similarly, your toddler will learn more quickly from 10 time-outs (see page 161) lasting 1 minute each than he will from 1 time-out that is 10 minutes long.

■ *Remain calm.* Regulate your own emotions to enhance toddler learning during discipline. Toddlers thrive on stimulation. If they can create excitement by misbehaving, they will. Display excitement and emotion when your toddler is behaving appropriately, but when your toddler misbehaves, keep your mouth closed and walk away unless he is in danger.

Specific Strategies for Installing Discipline

All toddler models require some amount of reprogramming to remove behavioral bugs in their systems. The section that follows presents numerous disciplinary approaches that are widely practiced and proven to work when used in combination with one another.

Whatever responses you choose to employ, it is important to use your methods consistently to send a clear message to your toddler. Before you begin the installation of the disciplinary program, discuss your strategies with any other toddler users to focus on specific problem behaviors and agree upon the methods you will use to address them.

Your toddler will learn more quickly if the consequence immediately follows the misbehavior and it clearly creates a difference from his normal situation. But even with immediate consequences that make a difference, it will take most toddlers numerous repetitions to learn appropriate behavior.

⚠ **EXPERT TIP:** *Verbal reasoning, warnings, and lengthy explanations of cause and effect or future consequences represent abstractions that are too difficult for toddlers to compute. Even toddlers who can verbalize the rules often do not demonstrate them with their behavior. Toddlers need their parents to take decisive action. Eventually, after many trials of combining words with consistent action, your child will respond to words alone.*

Differential Attention

Differential attention is a targeted, highly effective strategy of selectively ignoring the annoying behaviors you disapprove of and providing attention for those you do. Parents who work hard can become very

skillful in making quick, frequent switches between providing attention one moment and turning away the next. To practice differential attention, apply the following technique.

[1] Be on the alert for small instances of appropriate behavior you would like your toddler to increase (e.g., playing quietly or sitting calmly). Approach your toddler, describe his appropriate behavior out loud, and praise it. Imitate his appropriate behavior or actions (don't be afraid to be playful and goofy). Display affection, laugh, and get excited.

[2] Choose one annoying behavior you would like to address. When the toddler acts in this way, immediately switch from active attending to active ignoring (Fig. A). Look away from him, stop talking, or even walk away if necessary. Do not provide him with attention, positive or negative.

⚠ **EXPERT TIP:** *At first, your toddler may think that he has not displayed the annoying behavior fast enough, hard enough, or strangely enough for you to have noticed, so he may work even harder at it. This increased effort means that he noticed the difference in your response and your strategy is working.*

[3] After his increased efforts fail to gain your attention, he will try another tactic. If this tactic is irritating or annoying, continue to actively ignore him. He will eventually change strategies and behave correctly to get back your attention. When the change occurs, immediately return your full attention for any display of appropriate behavior (Fig. B).

[4] Repeat as necessary.

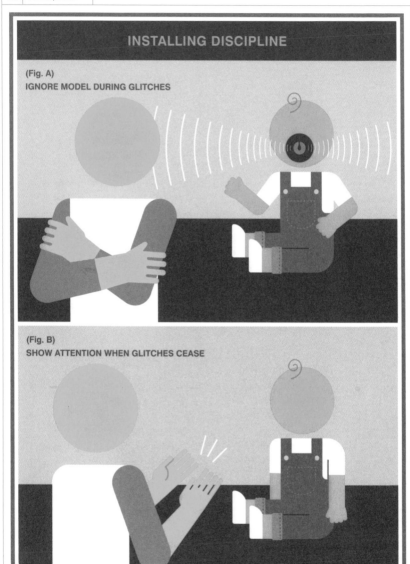

Verbal Warning

Verbally provide the toddler with a single short "if, then" statement that predicts the ensuing consequence if he doesn't self-correct his behavior. For example, "If you scream again, then you will have to go to your room." Another scream demands that you follow through on your warning, so don't threaten actions you are not willing to take. If he speaks more quietly, immediately provide positive feedback like verbal praise ("Thank you for speaking more softly; that's much better") or physical affection.

Prompt for Positive Behavior

Avoid constantly telling your toddler "no," "don't," and "quit." Instead, prompt for positive behavior by telling your toddler what you want him to do. You will decrease the negative interactions and increase positive interactions because you can reward him once he complies.

Toddlers are more likely to follow instructions that are phrased positively (e.g., "Please use your quiet voice" vs. "Stop yelling"). Here are some other examples of how you can use simple instructions to prompt positive alternatives to irritating or annoying behaviors.

DON'T SAY	SAY INSTEAD
"No running in the hall!"	"Walk, please."
"Stop blowing bubbles through the straw in your milk."	"Please use your straw for drinking."
"No jumping on the bed!"	"Please get off the bed."
"Stop running ahead of me."	"Please stay right next to me."

The "Do Over" or "Fix It"

This strategy is an offshoot of prompting for positive behavior, but it goes one step further by requiring the toddler to correct ("do over") or repair ("fix it") the damage incurred by the misbehavior. Examples of these types of instructions include "Please clean up your mess" or "Tell him you are sorry."

This strategy is especially helpful if your toddler completes an original request in a haphazard or hurried manner ("Oops, please come back and do that more carefully"), or if he's displaying an attitude ("Please do it again, this time more softly/quietly/nicely"). Without instigating a huge power struggle, the "do over" sends your toddler the simple message "Do it correctly the first time, and you won't have to do it again."

Removing an Offending Item

This may be the easiest yet most underutilized disciplinary strategy. If the toddler is using a toy or item in an annoying manner and you need a more immediate response than differential attention will provide, reach out and remove the item from her. Combine the response with a verbal warning to make it more effective.

For example, if your toddler is blowing bubbles through the straw in her glass of milk, begin by saying, "Please use your straw only for drinking." If she continues to blow bubbles, remove the straw. This may instigate whining, screaming, or crying by the toddler. Remain calm and ignore the tantrum. When the toddler self-calms and begins to eat quietly again, return the straw and repeat, "Please use your straw only for drinking." If the toddler follows your instructions, provide verbal and physical praise. If she ignores your instructions and begins to blow bubbles again, repeat the strategy from the beginning.

Time-Out

"Time-out" is short for "time-out from positive reinforcement," which refers to the characteristics of the toddler's surrounding environment.

In order to create time away from positive reinforcement, you must have a positively reinforcing environment in the first place. The environment outside of time-out is referred to as the "time-in" environment. The contrast between the time-in and time-out environments is the critical factor in making this strategy work. Time-outs work best in situations where your toddler is enjoying herself—for example, when she is playing outdoors, with new toys, or with friends. Other situations may be less reinforcing for many toddlers, such as when they are attending a lecture or are asked to remain alone in a quiet, dark room at bedtime.

Time-out is the most well-documented behavior reduction technique currently in use. Parents of toddlers report that the combination of time-in and time-out works much better than reasoning, lecturing, warning, threatening, yelling, and spanking. Unfortunately, time-out can be a difficult technique for parents to implement and a difficult consequence for some toddlers to accept. The following suggestions will help you implement this technique, but if after a few weeks of practice your toddler is still not responding to time-out, you may wish to consult a behavioral service provider.

[1] Establish a fun, enjoyable, and stimulating time-in environment. Use owner attention (see page 156) to catch her behaving appropriately.

[2] Don't yell, lecture, or show anger in response to misbehavior. Calmly and briefly state the infraction, followed by the consequence (e.g., "No hitting, time-out").

CREATIVE ERROR

MEALTIME MALFUNCTION

DEFECTIVE DISOBEDIENCE

TIME-OUT: This highly effective trouble-shooting solution entails removin

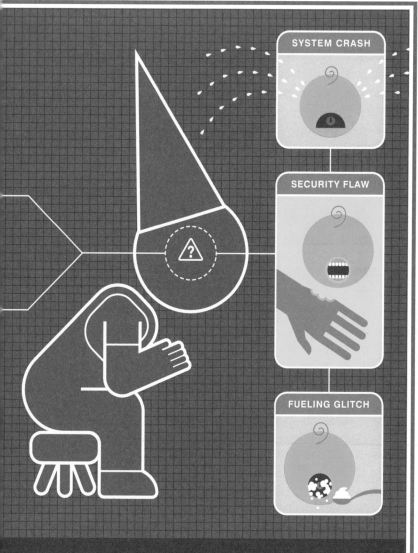

SYSTEM CRASH

SECURITY FLAW

FUELING GLITCH

the model from positively reinforced environments when an infraction occurs.

[3] Immediately separate the toddler from reinforcement by guiding her to the time-out location, such as a chair located in a safe but boring location. You may need to physically carry your toddler to time-out, or she may follow alongside you. The time-out location should be away from distractions such as television, radio, or toys. For young toddlers who cannot sit or refuse to sit in a chair, a portable playpen or crib with no toys or entertainment items can be used for time-out.

[4] While your toddler is serving time-out, do not look at, talk to, or interact with her in any way. The time-out should be as free from stimulation as possible.

EXPERT TIP: *Keep the first few time-outs very short to increase the likelihood of success. Gradually increase the duration of time-out to about 1 minute per year of age.*

[5] Once the time is up, the toddler must be quiet for 3 seconds before you release her from time-out.

[6] If your toddler went to time-out for refusing a request, repeat the instruction again. For example, as you approach her sitting in the chair, say, "Okay, you are quiet. You can come out. Now please put your blocks away."

[7] Reestablish time-in.

Spanking

Spanking occurs when a toddler user strikes the toddler's buttocks with an open hand, without using an object or causing injury. This disciplinary measure is best when used as a preplanned response to a persistent problem behavior that has not been remedied by other disciplinary efforts. It should never be used when a parent is angry or loses control. Although spanking has fallen out of favor, a large majority of parents continue to use it for some forms of toddler misbehavior. Spanking is more socially acceptable when used for a potentially dangerous behavior (e.g., running into the street) or to enforce toddler compliance with other disciplinary tactics like time-out.

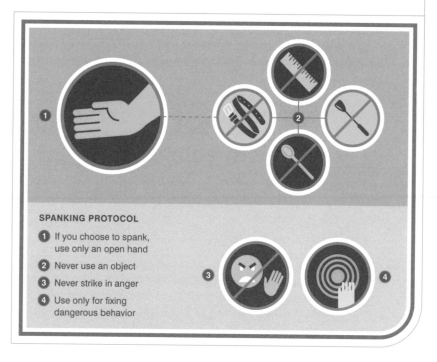

SPANKING PROTOCOL

1. If you choose to spank, use only an open hand
2. Never use an object
3. Never strike in anger
4. Use only for fixing dangerous behavior

Trouble-Shooting: Matching Disciplinary Techniques with Specific Misbehavior

In deciding upon an appropriate disciplinary tactic to match a toddler's misbehavior, ask yourself whether the toddler's behavior is dangerous, destructive, or harmful to the point of potential for injury to the toddler, another person, living being, or valued object.

If the answer to this question is yes, the toddler's behavior falls into Category A. Immediate parental action is necessary. See specific examples of behaviors and disciplinary actions from Category A on pages 167–168.

If the answer is no, your toddler's behavior falls into Category B. Your disciplinary options are more numerous and can be less forceful. These methods take longer to influence behavior, but they are less forceful and will minimize head-to-head battles. See specific examples of behaviors and disciplinary actions from Category B on pages 169–170.

⚠ *CAUTION: If the toddler has not yet learned to accept consequences or to self-calm, he may escalate from behavior in Category B to Category A, eventually becoming dangerous or destructive.*

Discipline for Category A Behaviors

Behavior:
BITING

Best discipline: Respond calmly and immediately. Place your toddler in time-out in a location where he can watch you applying first aid (wash the wound, apply an ice pack or cold cloth and then a bandage) and attending lovingly to the child who was bitten. Following release from time-out, the biter should apologize.

Once everything is calm again, consider any factor that you can address to reduce the future likelihood of biting. Toddlers often bite because they're tired, hungry, jealous, frustrated, seeking attention, or unable to find another way to express negative emotion.

EXPERT TIP: *Biting often starts innocently when a toddler is teething or using his mouth to explore a parent's shoulder. The immediate and dramatic verbal response ("Ouch!") catapults biting into a fascinating behavior. Over time, biting can become an effective tool to deter other toddlers from infringing on toys or space. Toddlers learn, often through being bitten themselves, that biting is quicker and more effective at affecting the behavior of other toddlers.*

Behavior:
HITTING, KICKING, PUSHING, PINCHING, OR THROWING TOYS

Best discipline: Immediate time-out. Say, "No hitting, time-out." Immediately following the time-out, the toddler must apologize to the person he hit, kicked, pushed, or pinched. If the aggressive behavior continues, send him back to time-out again to fine-tune his attitude.

Behavior:
THROWING FOOD

Best discipline: Immediate time-out. One option is to pull the chair away from the table or spin the highchair to face away from the table. Once the toddler is calm, instruct him to pick up the food and return to the table.

Persistent food throwing can be addressed by picking up your toddler's plate and ending the meal. Be sure to limit/restrict snacks so he is hungry by the next meal. Refer to Chapter 3: Feeding for further details.

Discipline for Category B Behaviors

Behavior:

TEMPER TANTRUM

Best discipline: Differential attention. Calmly ignore your toddler's inappropriate behavior, but respond quickly with your full attention when your toddler calms down. If the behavior escalates and becomes aggressive or destructive (hitting, throwing, banging head), use an immediate time-out.

Once a tantrum has begun, remain firm; giving in will only increase the prevalence of the behavior, as the toddler will learn that it is an effective way to get something she wants.

Prevention: Tantrums are a built-in programming bug in all toddler models that usually surfaces between the ages of 15 months and 3 years. Tantrums occur because the toddler's system is overloaded with the program upgrades that occur during this time. Take note of common triggers for temper tantrums—they are most likely to occur when a toddler is tired, bored, impatient, frustrated, hungry, or overwhelmed by demands. Keep the toddler's schedule realistic, and don't expect her to accomplish more than she can handle.

⚡ *EXPERT TIP: Toddlerhood brings many power struggles, so choose your battles based on their long-term importance. Give choices when appropriate and avoid saying no to everything without first thinking it over. If your toddler is intent on wearing her favorite shirt for the fourth day in a row, ask yourself whether it's worth the battle to make her change.*

If you say no but then change your mind, make sure you give in early, during low levels of inappropriate behavior. Never give in late or in response to highly inappropriate behavior just to make it stop.

Behavior:
WHINING

Best discipline: Differential attention. Ignore the toddler when she speaks in a whine, and present your full attention when she alters her tone. You can also calmly model (e.g., "Milk, please") in a lower voice and prompt ("Use your big girl voice to ask me") while still holding the desired item.

Think about common triggers for whining (is your toddler tired? bored?) or determine what behavior or skill the toddler needs to learn. If your toddler is whining for the unobtainable, see "Installing the Correct Response to 'No'" (page 171) and "Temper Tantrum" (page 169).

Prevention: Make sure your toddler's basic functions are being met—that she is well fed and rested and is receiving enough of your attention. Respond quickly when the toddler requests appropriately (even if by just making eye contact and prompting her to wait for a second). Don't just say no before thinking about whether the toddler's request is reasonable.

Installing Advanced Behavioral Functions

No punishment will teach a toddler the necessary skills to get along in the world. Effective discipline largely involves teaching appropriate behaviors and skills to overwrite irritating behaviors preinstalled in toddlers. Below you will find strategies for uploading critical skills toddlers need to successfully navigate their way toward preschool. Don't get frustrated if your toddler doesn't immediately display these skills, as they take time and effort to install. Remain patient and persistent, and you will see progress over time.

Installing the Correct Response to "No"

Words without action are virtually meaningless for toddlers. You will need to show him what "no" means and prove over and over that you really mean "no."

[1] If your toddler is getting into something nondangerous, calmly say "no" the first time. Don't obscure the word with a long explanation. Just say "no."

[2] If he continues, raise your voice to a sharp verbal reprimand.

[3] Further persistence with the forbidden behavior means he wants you to prove that he should stop. Physically remove the toddler from the area or remove the forbidden item from his reach.

[4] During the early phases of learning, any favorable response to "no" should earn praise and affection.

⚠ **EXPERT TIP:** *Saying "no" too often will cause the word to lose its meaning. Toddler-proof your home (see page 180) to limit the toddler's opportunity to get into circumstances that require a "no." For more minor infractions, use a positive request (i.e., "Sit on the couch, please") rather than a negative (i.e.,"No jumping on the couch").*

Saying "Please" and "Thank You"

Practice and repeated parental modeling will be necessary until these skills become fully functioning.

[1] Hold the desired item high in your hand while repeatedly modeling the correct request "please," prompting several times until your toddler imitates you.

[2] Immediately hand the item to him but keep it in your grasp until he says "thank you." You may need to prompt this response as well, by saying, "What do you say?" or "Remember to say thank you."

[3] Outright refusal to say "please" or "thank you" should result in cancellation of the transaction. Ignore the ensuing tantrum.

Waiting

Teaching your toddler how to wait will help him overcome his preinstalled desire for instant gratification.

[1] Ask your toddler to sit at the dinner table. Place an item (small toy, snack) of low to medium desirability in front of him.

[2] Set a timer for a few seconds and gently help him hold his hands in his lap. When the timer goes off or when you give the word, he can grab the toy or eat the food item. Praise immediately.

[3] Gradually increase the desirability of the item and lengthen the duration of waiting time, while fading out your assistance and presence.

[4] If he whines or persists at grabbing the item after several attempts, remove the item and try again later.

Taking Turns

Learning to take turns is one key to allocating scarce resources among more than one toddler (for example, toys in a toddler care center).

⚠ *CAUTION: Don't try to teach this skill using your toddler's favorite new toy.*

[1] Start with an easy task that allows your toddler to participate even when it's not her turn, like throwing or rolling a ball. Use words to label "your turn" and "my turn" each time you throw or catch.

[2] Move on to a task, like stacking blocks, that requires your toddler to wait passively for only a short time. Again, verbally label each person's turn.

[3] Progressively move toward games and activities that require longer periods of waiting while the other completes her turn.

[4] Set a timer for a few minutes to teach young toddlers to take turns playing alone with the most desirable toys.

⚠ **EXPERT TIP:** *It is perfectly normal for a toddler under the age of 2 to play alone while sitting next to another toddler. Experts call this "parallel play." Your toddler will most likely begin interactive play with other children around 30 months following delivery.*

Sharing

This function is difficult for the toddler to fully integrate, as all toddler models are preprogrammed to be concerned only with their own needs. But if you start slowly, teach by example, and praise any behavior that resembles sharing, this difficult skill can be mastered by age 3 or 4.

[1] Make your toddler aware of sharing efforts by naming the act. Praise your toddler for "sharing" when he voluntarily hands over a toy or item when he no longer wants it or is finished.

[2] Model your own sharing behavior and label it ("This frozen yogurt is really good. Here, I'll share it with you").

[3] Don't expect your toddler to share all of his toys. Allow him to identify and put away four or five "special" toys that are off-limits to siblings and visiting friends. All other toys should be available for others' use.

Self-Calming

Compared to toddlers who fuss, whine, and cry until a parent intervenes to give them what they want, a toddler who can self-calm is more likely to be productive in school, to become a good sport, and to make and keep friends. To install this valuable function, follow the strategy below.

ACTIVATING THE SHARING FUNCTION

TIPS TO ENCOURAGE SHARING

1. Teach sharing through example
2. Provide positive reinforcement when sharing occurs
3. Allow toddler several "non-sharing" toys

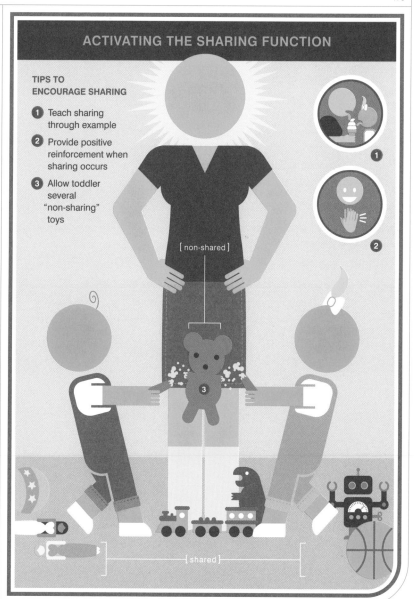

[non-shared]

[shared]

[1] Maintain control and remain calm yourself. Don't argue or scream yourself, or your toddler will imitate your behavior.

[2] Don't hold, hug, rock, soothe, or verbally reassure your toddler during tantrums. Even if you are tempted to immediately put an end to an annoyance, in the long run your actions will only provoke further tantrums and block your toddler's development of self-control functions. Remind yourself that the more intensely he reacts, the quicker the tantrum will be over, because the body isn't physically capable of intense reactions for long durations.

EXPERT TIP: *When your toddler's coping skills are overwhelmed and he is scared, highly anxious, sick, or injured, lend a great deal of comfort and reassurance. However, when he is simply angry because life is not going his way, practice selective ignoring to help him learn to get over it.*

[3] Immediately return to talking and interacting with him in a positive manner once he calms.

Following Simple Instructions

Teaching your toddler to comply with simple instructions can be helpful to you in managing his behavior. Learning to follow instructions readies the toddler to acquire more difficult life skills like self–waste disposal, eating, dressing, and following rules in public situations.

[1] Start with very simple instructions that you are certain your toddler understands and is capable of performing. Examples include "come here," "stand up," "sit down," "pick up," "hand me," and "open the door."

[2] Establish eye contact with your child, call his name, and give the instruction only one time, loud and clear. For example, say "John, please come here." Add hand gestures if you think your toddler does not understand the words.

[3] If your toddler complies, say "Good boy! You came when I called you!" Display positive cues, such as a smile, and add physical affection, such as a hug or pat on the head.

⚠ **EXPERT TIP:** *Praise, enthusiasm, and affection should be reserved for those times when your toddler complies without physical guidance.*

[4] If your toddler does not comply with your instruction within five seconds (ignores you, stalls, asks a question, makes an excuse) or does something other than what you asked, physically guide him through the requested task. For example, if you asked your child to sit down, gently take his hand, walk him to the chair, and guide him to sit. Use only as much physical contact as necessary to gain compliance, and gradually eliminate your assistance so he learns to comply with the instruction on his own.

[5] Do not give another instruction until the first one has been followed.

[6] If your toddler starts crying or becomes aggressive, you can either ignore the behavior or use a brief time-out (see page 161). Once he has calmed down, repeat the instruction.

Chapter 8

Safety and Emergency Maintenance

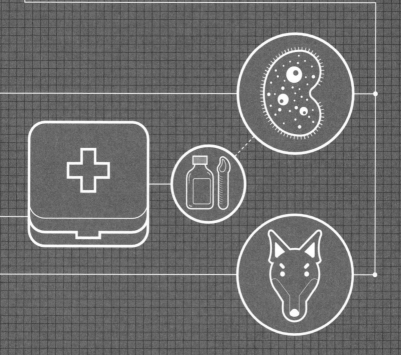

Childproofing the Toddler's Environment

As your baby upgrades to a toddler, her new level of mobility and curiosity will require continual adjustments to your living quarters to ensure her safety.

General Strategies

Many toddlers will begin to explore the environment above them—by either pulling or climbing up—and you should begin your focus there as well. To get the best perspective, crawl throughout the house on your hands and knees to see the environment at the same level as your toddler.

[1] Cover electrical outlets and secure electrical cords. Use safety plugs to restrict access to unused outlets, and place lamp and appliance cords behind heavy furniture or use cord shorteners.

[2] Install doorstops on all interior doors to keep doors from opening and closing all the way, to keep a door from closing on toddler fingers or locking your toddler in a room.

[3] Install locks on all windows and keep them locked or opened only from the top.

[4] Place large, bright stickers on glass doors and large windows to make them visible to your toddler (so she won't try to walk right through).

[5] Coil all window shade strings out of reach to avoid a strangulation hazard.

[6] Install gates across stairways and in the doorways of off-limit rooms. Pressure release gates should be placed only at the bottom of stairs—use fixed gates at the top of stairs.

[7] Secure bookcases and cabinets to the wall with L-brackets. If your toddler pulls herself up by holding one of these objects, she could pull the furniture down onto herself if it is not secure.

[8] Dispose of poisonous houseplants, and move all other plants and flowers out of your toddler's reach. Be sure to pick up any dead leaves as soon as you see them.

EXPERT TIP: When traveling, use the same standards you apply at home to secure your living quarters. Put together a small travel package of childproofing tools that includes several outlet covers, curtain cord ties, and temporary cabinet drawer latches.

[9] Vacuum carpets and floors frequently to remove dust, dirt, and potential choking hazards.

[10] Install a smoke detector on each level of your living space, outside of bedrooms, and near the kitchen. Change batteries in fire safety devices and carbon monoxide detectors at least once every six months. Keep a fire extinguisher out of your toddler's reach near the kitchen and fireplace.

[11] Secure heating vents and cold-air returns. Install plastic shields on hot-air vents to prevent burns. If the cold-air return is built into the floor, make sure that it can support the weight of your toddler.

[12] Remove firearms from the home, or secure them, unloaded, in a locked, hidden box. Store ammunition in a separate, locked location.

[13] Place corner bumpers around tables, windowsills, hearths, or any other sharp furniture edges.

[14] Place all matches, chemicals, alcohol, plastic bags, and sharp knives out of reach or locked in cabinets. Hide small items that could be swallowed, like buttons, marbles, coins, paper clips, and safety pins.

[15] Secure pet doors so that a toddler may not crawl outside unattended.

Bedroom Strategies

[1] When switching the toddler to a toddler bed (see page 78), install appropriate bed rails to secure the toddler in place when he is in sleep mode.

[2] Keep the area under the toddler's bed free of materials (large boxes, heavy blankets) that could trap the toddler underneath. Check for small choking hazards.

[3] Place the bed away from glass windows and curtain cords.

[4] Latch dresser drawers so that they stop before pulling all the way out.

[5] Replace closet or bedroom door latches with push-type latches that may be easily opened from inside.

Bathroom Strategies

Never allow your toddler to enter the bathroom unattended, even when you are training her for self–waste disposal.

[1] Confirm that all medicines, including vitamins and over-the-counter remedies, and cleaning supplies are safely locked in an out-of-reach cabinet.

[2] Install a rubber mat in the bathtub and a standard nonskid bath mat for tiled or hardwood surfaces.

[3] Cover bathtub faucet fixtures with a rubber cover to protect the toddler's head from injury but continue to allow water to flow through.

[4] Never leave the bathtub full of water. Drain it immediately after removing your toddler from the bath.

[5] Install ground fault circuit interrupter (GFCI) outlets. These outlets will break the circuit, cutting off power, if the outlet becomes wet or overloaded.

[6] Install a toilet seat lock. Get in the habit of closing the toilet seat and lid. As your toddler matures and you reprogram her for self–waste disposal, this safety feature will become obsolete.

[7] Do not dispose of potentially harmful materials (razor blades, expired medicines, toiletry bottles) in an open bathroom waste bin.

[8] Ensure that the household water heater is set below 120 degrees Fahrenheit (48.9°C).

[9] Unplug and store safely away all hair dryers, curling irons, and other appliances when not in use.

Kitchen Strategies

[1] Do not leave the kitchen unattended when food is cooking on the stove or in the oven.

[2] Put all knives, sharp utensils, and plastic bags in a locked drawer. Keep glasses and heavy plates out of reach.

[3] Install knob and stove guards and safety latches on all drawers and cupboards. If your toddler is able to open the safety latches, remove any sharp or dangerous utensils to an out-of-reach location.

[4] Move chairs and step stools away from cooking surfaces.

[5] Use the rear burners first when using the stove. Turn all pot handles toward the back of the stove.

EXPERT TIP: *Create a toddler-safe cupboard that the toddler can explore. Fill it with plastic containers, wooden spoons, small pots and pans, and other toddler-safe items. Change the contents every few weeks to maintain your toddler's interest and to distract your toddler's attention from more dangerous areas of the kitchen.*

[6] Unplug and secure all appliances when not in use. If you have an early model refrigerator, install a fridge latch that allows the door to open from the inside or lock from the outside.

[7] Place hot materials safely back from the edge of countertops.

[8] Do not carry a toddler and hot food or drink simultaneously.

Living/Dining Room Strategies

[1] Lock or place safely out of reach any breakable items—glassware, china, objets d'art, and so forth.

[2] Avoid the use of place mats and tablecloths or tie up the corners of a tablecloth so the toddler cannot pull them down on top of himself.

[3] Place televisions safely. Strap a television firmly to its surface and/or store the TV as low and far back as possible.

[4] Secure the fireplace. Install grills to restrict the toddler's access. Remove and store any keys or knobs that operate a gas fireplace. Remove fireplace tools.

Outdoor Strategies

Never leave your toddler unattended when he is in the yard. Be especially watchful of your toddler near swimming pools, ponds, creeks, and other water; a toddler can drown in just 1 to 2 inches (2.5–5 cm) of water.

[1] Enclose swimming pools or ponds on all sides by a securely locking fence. Remain vigilant when your toddler is near the water—do not attempt to accomplish any other task than to watch your toddler at these times.

[2] Always put gardening and mowing tools and chemicals away when you are done using them. Never leave a toddler unattended in the yard, especially when these items are within his reach.

[3] Install locks on any yard gates, sheds, or garage doors.

⚠ *CAUTION: Store buckets and other containers with the opening facing the ground so they do not collect rainwater. Buckets are a particular danger because toddlers' upper bodies and heads are heavier than their lower bodies; if a toddler leans into a bucket and falls over, he may be unable to stand up again.*

[4] Cover outdoor electrical outlets and test GFCI outlets. Always unplug electrical yard tools when they are not in use.

[5] Keep toddlers out of the area when mowing, trimming, or chemically treating the yard. Confirm how long you should keep a toddler from the area after any fertilizers or chemical treatments are applied.

[6] Keep outdoor grills out of reach of toddlers.

[7] Maintain fences and trees in the yard. Be sure that fence panels are secure and that any dead or hanging branches have been trimmed.

[8] Remove all poisonous plants from the areas where your child plays.

The Heimlich Maneuver and Cardiopulmonary Resuscitation (CPR)

If your toddler's airway becomes obstructed by an object, the Heimlich maneuver can be used to remove it. If your toddler's breathing has stopped, CPR may be used to restore it. All primary and secondary care providers should be trained in both procedures. Contact your local health agency about training.

Identifying Respiratory Problems

[1] Watch for warning signs. Is the toddler having difficulty breathing? Is the toddler turning blue? Is the toddler choking, unconscious, or unresponsive to stimulus?

⚠ EXPERT TIP: You can usually listen and/or feel to see if the toddler is breathing. Alternatively, hold an unbreakable mirror up to the nose and mouth of the toddler. The mirror will fog if the toddler is breathing.

[2] Instruct someone to call emergency paramedics. If you are alone, proceed with the Heimlich maneuver or CPR for one minute; then call and return to the toddler.

[3] Evaluate the problem. Is the toddler not breathing? Is she in the middle of a meal? Could an object be lodged in her throat? If so, perform the Heimlich maneuver (see page 188).

Is the toddler's breathing only partially impeded? Can you hear wheezing, gagging, or coughing? If so, sit the toddler forward and allow her to try to clear the obstruction through the natural reflexes of coughing and gagging. If choking persists after two or three minutes, seek emergency assistance. Do not perform the Heimlich maneuver in this situation because you risk lodging the object further.

If the toddler is unconscious but does not seem to have an obstruction in her airway, perform CPR (see page 190).

If the toddler is currently sick, or if the toddler has allergies that might affect her ability to breathe, do not perform the Heimlich maneuver or CPR; call emergency paramedics immediately and follow their instructions.

Performing the Heimlich Maneuver

Use the following technique for toddlers between the ages of 1 and 3.

[1] Lay the toddler on a flat, hard surface (such as the floor or a solid table).

[2] Kneel down and straddle your toddler's thighs. Do not rest your weight on your toddler's legs.

[3] Set the heel of one hand on the toddler's abdomen, between his navel and the bottom of his rib cage. Place the other hand on top of the first.

[4] Press firmly, but gently, both inward and upward. At a rapid pace, apply five to six thrusts.

[5] Check the toddler's mouth for any objects and remove carefully. Do not sweep the mouth or attempt to remove any object that you cannot see or can only partially see. This may lodge the object farther back in the toddler's throat.

PERFORMING THE HEIMLICH MANEUVER

HEIMLICH PROTOCOL

1. Lay toddler on flat, hard surface
2. Press firmly five to six times
3. Check mouth for foreign objects. If none are found, return to step 2 until object is dislodged

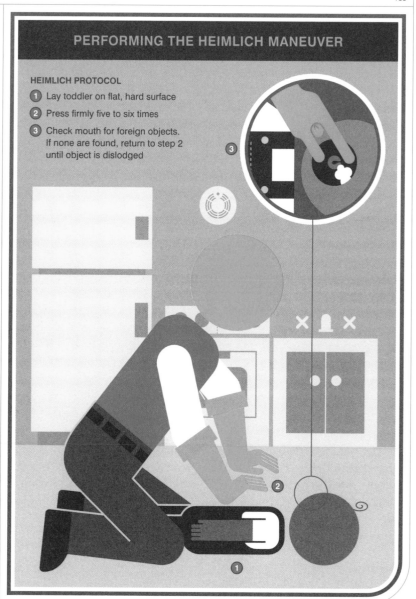

[6] Repeat steps 1 through 5 until the obstruction is clear of the throat and removed from the toddler's mouth.

[7] Check the toddler's breathing and perform CPR (see below) if necessary.

Performing Cardiopulmonary Resuscitation (CPR)

Use the following technique for toddlers between the ages of 1 and 3.

[1] Lay the toddler on a firm, flat surface (such as a floor or solid table).

[2] Tilt the toddler's head back slightly to open his airway (Fig. A). Press down gently on his forehead as you lift the toddler's chin slightly.

[3] Place your mouth over your toddler's nose and mouth. If you cannot completely cover your toddler's nose and mouth with your own, pinch his nostrils closed gently but tightly with one hand.

[4] Deliver two light breaths into your toddler's lungs (Fig. B). As you blow, check to be sure that the toddler's chest is rising and air is getting into his lungs. If you cannot see his chest rise, perform the Heimlich maneuver (see page 188) if there is an obstruction and then repeat steps 1 through 4.

[5] Check the toddler's breathing. If he is breathing on his own, wait for the emergency paramedics to arrive. If he is still not breathing, check for a pulse. Press your index and middle fingers lightly on the toddler's neck (on either side under his jaw) and feel for a pulse (Fig. C).

PERFORMING CARDIOPULMONARY RESUSCITATION

(Fig. A)
RAISE CHIN

(Fig. B)
DELIVER OXYGEN

x3

(Fig. C)
CHECK PULSE

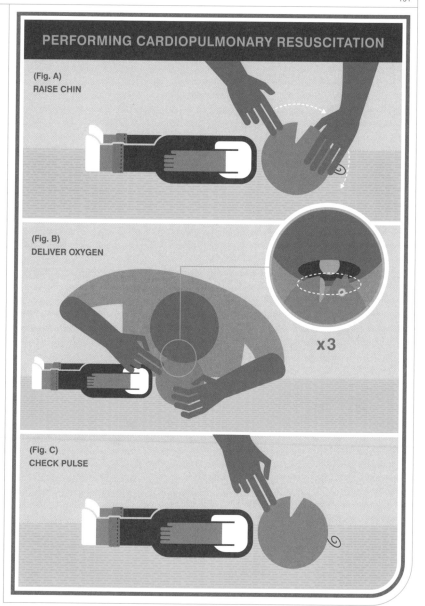

[6] If you feel a pulse but the toddler is not breathing, repeat step 4 for one minute—delivering breaths at a rate of 20 per minute (about 1 breath per 3 seconds). Check the toddler's breathing after each 2 breaths. If you do not feel a pulse, proceed to step 7.

[7] Place the heel of one hand on your toddler's sternum (breastbone). Place the hand so that the heel runs vertically up the sternum from just above the base of the bone to just at the nipples.

[8] Compress the chest 1 to $1^1/_2$ inches (2.5–4 cm), 4 to $4^1/_2$ times in a 3-second span.

[9] After each fifth compression, deliver one breath as above.

[10] Check the toddler's breathing and pulse. If they are restored, proceed to step 12.

[11] Continue performing CPR at the rate of 80 to 100 compressions per minute. Deliver a breath after every fifth compression. Repeat until emergency paramedics arrive.

[12] After the toddler is resuscitated, visit the emergency room to confirm function and lack of injury.

Measuring the Toddler's Core Temperature

A toddler's core temperature should be 98.6 degrees Fahrenheit (37°C). Though toddler upgrades include more advanced motor and listening skills, oral temperature measurements still will not be as effective as rectal or armpit temperature readings.

⚠ *CAUTION: It is advisable to use a digital thermometer when measuring the toddler's core temperature. Glass thermometers are best avoided as they may break.*

[1] Prepare the thermometer. Rinse the tip of the thermometer with warm water and lubricate with petroleum jelly.

[2] Undress the toddler and direct him to lie on his belly.

[3] Insert the thermometer no more than 1 inch (2.5 cm) into the toddler's rectum.

⚠ *CAUTION: A toddler's new mobility may allow him to squirm or roll around. Attempt to keep the toddler as still as possible and console him in his discomfort. If movement becomes unmanageable, remove the thermometer, find another adult to assist you, and repeat steps 1 through 3.*

[4] Hold the thermometer in place until the temperature registers. Most digital thermometers will audibly announce when the core temperature has been read (usually after about 2 minutes).

[5] Remove the thermometer and read the temperature.

[6] If the toddler's core temperature is above 103.5 degrees Fahrenheit (39.7°C), contact his service provider.

⚠ **EXPERT TIP:** *You may also choose to measure your toddler's core temperature by placing a digital thermometer under his armpit and keeping his arm pressed to his side. Temperatures measured in this manner are generally 1 degree Fahrenheit (.05˚C) less than actual core temperatures.*

Delivering Medicine to the Toddler

All toddlers—even those with updated software—are prone to viruses. Occasionally, you will need to download medicine into your toddler to bring his functioning back to full capacity. Many toddler models are resistant to medication installation. Use the following procedures to assist your input.

Liquid and Elixir Delivery

Use liquids for all units, as toddlers are generally unable to swallow pills until they are 6 to 8 years old. Chewable pills, if a manufacturer offers such a format, are acceptable.

[1] Secure your medication and a proper delivery device. You may use a liquid syringe, a medicine cup, a medicine spoon, or a pacifier medicine dispenser. All of these devices should have multiple markings for measuring dosages.

⚠ **CAUTION:** *Do not use a household teaspoon or tablespoon to administer medicine. The actual amount these items can hold varies greatly from model to model.*

[2] Measure the proper dosage. If the liquid is thick, you may get a more accurate dose when using a syringe. When using a measuring medicine cup, some of the liquid may stick to the sides and deliver a smaller dose to the toddler.

⚠ **CAUTION:** *Whether the medicine is prescribed or purchased over the counter, your service provider or the manufacturer will provide an acceptable dosage. Generally, dosage is based on a toddler's weight rather than his age. However, if your toddler weighs more or less than a manufacturer recommends for his age group, consult your service provider regarding proper dosage.*

[3] Feed the toddler, if necessary. Many medications, especially antibiotics, require that the medication be administered on a full stomach, or at least with food. Check with your pharmaceutical service provider or read the manufacturer's instructions.

[4] Approach the toddler in a positive manner and present the delivery device for medicinal consumption.

[5] Deliver the medicine to the back of the toddler's throat or into his cheeks to aid in consumption and to reduce the toddler's ability to taste or spit out the medicine.

⚠ **EXPERT TIP:** *Consult your service provider if you believe you overdosed or underdosed your toddler.*

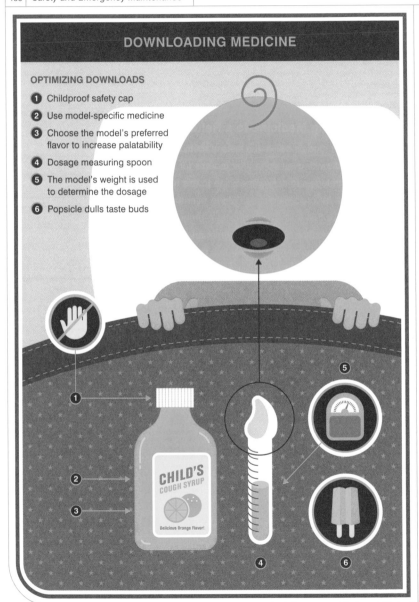

DOWNLOADING MEDICINE

OPTIMIZING DOWNLOADS

1. Childproof safety cap
2. Use model-specific medicine
3. Choose the model's preferred flavor to increase palatability
4. Dosage measuring spoon
5. The model's weight is used to determine the dosage
6. Popsicle dulls taste buds

CHILD'S COUGH SYRUP

Delicious Orange Flavor!

[6] Offer the toddler a drink to wash the medicine into the stomach for absorption.

Downloading Medicine to a Reluctant Toddler

Many toddler models dislike the taste of medicines, and as a result they refuse to swallow or even open their mouths for medicinal delivery. Use the following strategies to deliver medicine to this type of model.

■ Purchase flavored medicines. Many over-the-counter medications are sold in flavors that appeal to toddlers. A pharmacist can also flavor antibiotics when he or she mixes them. Aftermarket flavorings may also be purchased at your local retailer, though these may affect the amount of medicine you will need to deliver; consult the label of the flavoring for usage instructions.

■ Explain to your toddler why he has to take medication. Some toddlers appreciate the reasoning behind an undesirable action and will then follow your instructions.

⚠ *CAUTION: Do not refer to medicine as candy to make your toddler more enthusiastic about taking it. Your toddler may seek out the medicine and overdose himself when you are not paying attention.*

■ Surround medicinal delivery with a flavorful food or drink. For example, offer a toddler a bite of his favorite food, deliver the medicine, and then offer a drink of his favorite beverage.

■ Give your toddler a Popsicle prior to delivering medicine. The cold will dull his taste buds and lessen the flavor of the medication.

■ Depending on your model of toddler, offer the medication in one full squirt, or several smaller squirts of a single dose.

Toddler Medical Maintenance

Most toddler models will continue to experience general illnesses similar to those experienced when the unit was a baby. Continue your common practice of treating these illnesses in addition to contacting the toddler's service provider. Additionally, your toddler may experience several incidents of illness and injury due to her new level of activity and her age. Contact the toddler's service provider if your toddler shows any signs of malfunction.

 ## Animal Injuries

Dog bites and cat scratches are conditions that affect your toddler's exposed extremities as a result of aggressive contact with a dog or a cat. Both conditions should be treated and watched.

Symptoms of dog bites may include puncture marks, bleeding, and bruising around the area of contact. Determine whether the offending animal is current on all shots and contact the toddler's service provider for a recommended course of action. Generally, in the case of minor bites, clean the affected area and use antibiotic ointment and bandages to treat the wound. Watch for signs of infection, which might include redness, swelling, and drainage of the area; if these symptoms occur, call your toddler's service provider. The wound should resolve in seven to ten days.

Symptoms of cat scratches include scratch marks and swelling at the area of contact. Clean the area well and use antibiotic ointment and bandages to treat the wound. In some cases, a toddler may contract cat scratch fever from a cat scratch. Symptoms of this illness include swollen glands in the neck and fever. Contact your service provider for a recommended course of action. Cat scratches and cat scratch fever (when treated) should resolve in about a week.

Bee Stings

Bee stings are generally a serious concern only if an allergic reaction occurs. Symptoms of a severe reaction include abdominal pain, vomiting, difficulty breathing, and/or hives (in a location other than that of the bite). Contact the toddler's service provider immediately at the first sign of severe reaction. Mild reactions (such as itching or slight swelling at the site of the sting) may be treated as follows.

[1] Remove the stinger by pushing your fingernail across the skin and pressing the stinger straight out. Using tweezers or pinching with your fingers to remove the stinger may release more venom.

[2] Wrap a cold compress in a towel and hold it to the site of the sting for 5 to 15 minutes.

[3] Apply cortisone cream to the site.

[4] Watch for swelling or severe allergic reaction. Such a reaction may appear in as little as a few minutes, or in as long as six hours.

Broken Bones

Sometimes a fall, movement, or impact is rough enough to crack one of your toddler's bones. The combination of the toddler's developing skeletal system and physical abilities puts him more at risk of broken bones than younger and older units.

Symptoms of broken bones include bruising, an obvious deformity of the bone, and point tenderness (pain in a specific, focused point).

However, the most common toddler fractures are hairline fractures that may only show point tenderness. If a toddler is using a hand, foot, arm, or leg in an unusual manner or has a bruise that does not resolve, gently feel along the area and note if the toddler experiences any point tenderness. If he does, contact the toddler's service provider, who may schedule an X-ray examination.

Bumps and Bruises

The incidence of bruising increases exponentially as your unit upgrades from helpless infant to active toddler. Large, purple bruises found on a toddler's body are hematomas—collections of blood and fluids at the site of an injury. Bruising may indicate injury as serious as a broken bone (see above) or as minor as a topical bump.

Bruises are generally found on a toddler's lower extremities and arms, but they may appear anywhere on the body. Often, as a result of a toddler's frequent bruising, a bruise may appear to move from place to place on a toddler's body. In fact, these are multiple bruises both appearing and resolving in different areas. Additionally, blood may collect in a lower part of a toddler's injured body (for example, bruising at the elbow may cause swelling at the wrist). Treat bruises as follows.

[1] Place an ice pack on the injured area as soon as you can. This will inhibit both bruising and swelling.

[2] Watch the bruise over the next few days. Bruises may turn hard and get calcified, but these types of bruises should resolve in a month or possibly two. Bruises may also turn red and/or warm, which would suggest a

secondary infection. Contact your toddler's service provider with any concerns or if your toddler's bruise does not resolve in three to five days.

⚠ **EXPERT TIP:** *Bruising on the head may lead to purple-colored swelling under the eyes. This is a common result of head injury and is not necessarily cause for concern unless the symptoms discussed below, under "Head Injuries," are recognized.*

Burns

Burns are caused when a toddler touches a heated surface or is exposed, unprotected, to the sun for extended periods. First-degree burns are minor burns that are red and painful. Second-degree burns are more serious and are often red, painful, and blistered. Third-degree burns (blistered burns with not much pain associated) are most serious and should be treated immediately by emergency service personnel.

To treat first- or second-degree burns

[1] Place the affected area into cold water for about 10 minutes to cut down on swelling, redness, and blistering. Do not use ice to treat a burn.

[2] Place cool washcloths over the affected area for several minutes.

[3] Allow the area to air-dry. Do not pat dry with a towel.

[4] Apply antibiotic cream, burn cream, or aloe vera to the area. Do not apply oil, butter, or ointment.

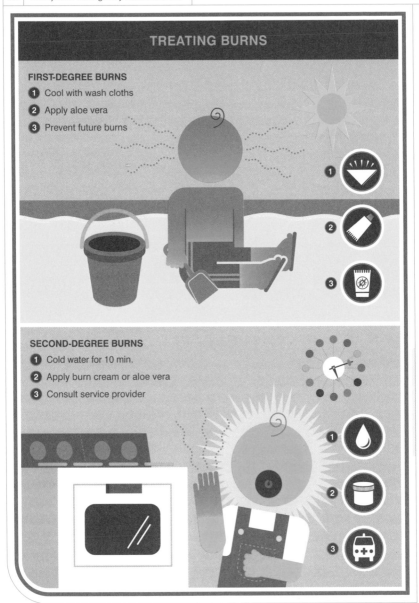

TREATING BURNS

FIRST-DEGREE BURNS
1. Cool with wash cloths
2. Apply aloe vera
3. Prevent future burns

SECOND-DEGREE BURNS
1. Cold water for 10 min.
2. Apply burn cream or aloe vera
3. Consult service provider

[5] Cover with a sterile, nonadhesive dressing. Keep the area both clean and dry for a week to 10 days, or until the burn heals.

Cuts and Scrapes

Cuts and scrapes are the result of any minor trauma to your toddler's skin that causes bleeding or scratches. Wash the area with soap and water, clean any debris from the cut or scrape, and apply direct pressure with a clean cloth until the bleeding subsides. Many toddlers react well to the application of a small bandage (especially when the bandage is adorned with your toddler's favorite animated characters), but when possible, leave the cut or scrape exposed to the air for faster healing. Apply antibiotic ointment whenever a cut or scrape fails to show signs of healing within a few days.

Dental Trauma

Broken or loose teeth from some form of oral trauma (such as a fall from a bike or down the stairs) are generally not harmful to the toddler as long as the tooth remains attached to the gums, but a trip to the dental service provider is recommended. If a tooth falls out or is knocked from your toddler's mouth, apply pressure to the area to stop the bleeding, locate the tooth, and consult your toddler's dental service provider immediately.

EXPERT TIP: Place a wet tea bag—preferably caffeine free—on a toddler's bleeding gums or tooth socket to help stop bleeding.

Ear Infections

Ear infections are the result of a viral or bacterial infection in the middle ear. Mild ear infections can last from three to five days or can recur for several weeks. If an ear infection lasts for more than five days, consult the toddler's service provider.

Symptoms of an ear infection include inconsolable crying, grabbing at the ear, distress upon changing positions (i.e., from vertical to horizontal), and fever. If you suspect the toddler is suffering from an ear infection, contact the toddler's service provider.

Ear infections are generally treated with antibiotics. This is the quickest cure for the infection and will prevent the infection from spreading and causing more serious problems, like meningitis. Different antibiotics are compatible with different toddler models. Several different kinds of antibiotics could be prescribed before a match is found. If your toddler experienced ear infections as a baby, your service provider may prescribe a previously successful antibiotic. To maintain a balance of good stomach bacteria, feed the toddler yogurt while he is on the course of antibiotics.

EXPERT TIP: Use an eyedropper to apply one drop of olive oil to the outside edge of each of your toddler's ear canals. Allow the oil to work its way into each canal. This may provide some temporary relief for the toddler's pain.

Eczema

Eczema is a skin condition common in toddlers. Symptoms of eczema include redness, scaling, itching, dryness, bumps, and blisters on the skin. It is most frequently found behind the toddler's knees and elbows, or on the unit's face. To treat eczema:

[1] Apply toddler-appropriate hydrocortisone cream twice a day to the affected area.

[2] Decrease the frequency of toddler bathing. Bathe the toddler no more than every other day.

[3] Apply moisturizing lotion to the area while it is still damp.

Electric Shock

Curious, active toddlers are most at risk of experiencing electric shock from touching wall outlets and biting on electric cords. Take measures to protect your toddler from these dangers (see page 180). If your toddler inserts a metal object into a wall outlet or touches a current, she will likely move away from the current quickly enough to avoid serious injury, and you may not even know about the incident. If you suspect that your toddler has been electrocuted, check her for burns. You may see third-degree burns such as a blackened mark at the point of contact or at a point of exit (this may appear anywhere on a toddler's body), or you may see less serious first- and second-degree burns as evidenced by blisters, redness, or swelling (see page 201 for advice on burn treatment).

If your toddler experiences a more severe shock, such as a shock from biting an electrical cord, she may be knocked unconscious and her heart may stop beating. In this case, immediately cut off the power supply, call emergency services, and then administer CPR (see page 190).

⚠ *CAUTION: Contact a service provider immediately for any type of electrical shock—even a minor burn may cause a serious internal injury.*

Fever

Most service providers believe that low-grade fevers are beneficial to the toddler, as fevers are a sign that the toddler's immune system is battling illness and slowing viral replication. This keeps the toddler from getting sicker. As a result, many service providers do not recommend treating a fever under 101 degrees Fahrenheit (38.3°C).

⚠ *CAUTION: If your 1- to 4-year-old model has a fever higher than 103.5 degrees Fahrenheit (39.7°C), contact the toddler's service provider.*

[1] Feel the toddler's forehead and back. If it is warm to the touch, take her core temperature (see page 193). Note that a toddler's temperature may normally be slightly higher right after naps or bedtime.

[2] If the toddler's temperature is between 101 and 103 degrees Fahrenheit (38.3–39.4°C), treat the fever with an accurate dose of ibuprofen and/or contact the toddler's service provider. Continue dosage of ibuprofen as recommended by the service provider until the fever subsides.

[3] If the toddler's temperature is above 103.5 degrees Fahrenheit (39.7°C), contact the service provider immediately. Sponge or bathe the toddler with warm water. Do not use cold water, as it may cause the toddler to shiver.

Food Allergies

Although rare, a toddler may experience an allergy to particular foods. Generally, food allergies are inherited, so if either parent has a food allergy, consult your service provider before introducing these same foods to your toddler. Within an hour

after consumption, symptoms may include rash, wheezing, or fainting. If you suspect a food allergy, consult your service provider and a nutritionist and/or allergist to determine an accurate diagnosis. Generally food allergies are treated by removing those foods from your toddler's diet. Once diagnosed, pay attention to the ingredients in a particular food before delivering it to your toddler.

The most common food allergies include:

- Milk
- Eggs
- Peanuts and other nuts
- Strawberries
- Fish and shellfish
- Wheat
- Soy

EXPERT TIP: *Many toddlers will outgrow a food allergy by the time they reach first grade.*

Head Injuries

Head injuries are common with active but less coordinated toddlers. Such injuries should be treated with an ice pack to reduce swelling and by consulting your service provider. If your toddler experiences a head injury but is still conscious, evaluate his condition and contact your toddler's service provider if he displays any of the following malfunctions:

- Pupils not the same size when a light is shined into the eyes
- Vomiting
- Lethargy or somnolence (sleepiness) so that you have difficulty rousing him
- Persistent lump or bruise on the area of impact

⚠ **CAUTION:** *If your toddler experiences a head injury that causes unconsciousness, contact your emergency service provider immediately.*

Impaired Vision

Many toddler models experience a malfunction with their visual sensors that requires corrective lenses. The most common types of visual impairment found in toddler models are:

■ Myopia, or nearsightedness, which causes difficulty clearly seeing objects that are faraway

■ Hyperopia, or farsightedness, which causes difficulty clearly seeing objects that are close

■ Amblyopia, or lazy eye, which will cause one of your toddler's eyes to drift while the other stays fixed

When analyzing your toddler's vision, consider the following:

■ If both toddler owners are myopic, there is a good chance the toddler will be as well.

■ Note your toddler's relative position to the television or to books as you read them.

■ Pick an object in the distance and point it out to your toddler. Attempt to gain confirmation that the toddler can see it.

■ Pick an object that is closer and point it out to your toddler. Attempt to gain confirmation that the toddler can see it clearly.

If your toddler's vision seems impaired in one of the above manners, consult a vision service provider.

Lice

Your toddler is more likely to experience head or body lice once he is visiting a preschool or day care provider on a regular basis. Head lice have white nits (eggs) that are deposited on the hair shaft. Body lice create scabs on the body that can look like any number of different rashes. Both conditions cause itching and both are transferable to human beings. If your toddler contracts lice:

[1] Treat itchy areas with diphenhydramine.

[2] Consult your service provider and secure a course of lice shampoos and soap—these may be either over-the-counter or prescription. Treat every member of the family, though it is not necessary to treat pets.

[3] Wash all sheets, bedding, and clothing in extremely hot water regularly until lice incidence has subsided. If there are pillows, dry-clean-only clothes, or other unwashable fabric-covered items, seal them in plastic bags for two weeks to kill the lice. Vacuum all rugs in the house to get rid of infected hair that may have fallen to the floor.

Poison Control

Toddlers can be at a high risk for poisoning. Use the childproofing strategies (see page 180) to remove poisons from your toddler's reach.

If you suspect that your toddler has ingested a poison, contact your local poison control center immediately. Memorize or keep the number posted near every phone in the home. Have the ingredients of the substance close at hand and follow their instructions.

Common Poisons in the Home

Below you will find some of the more common possible poisons found in your home. Obtain a more complete list from your pediatrician or poison control center and lock these items securely away.

- Alcohol (liquor, some mouthwashes, and rubbing alcohol)
- Perfume, nail polish remover, hair spray, skin lotions and creams, shaving creams, and topical ointments
- Nutmeg and some spices, cooking wines and vinegars, tenderizers, and flavor extracts
- Cigarettes and tobacco in general
- Fertilizers and some common houseplants and garden plants
- Medications and supplements
- Cleaning supplies and solutions
- Household glues and paints

Poison Ivy

If the oil of the poison ivy plant comes into contact with your toddler's skin, it will cause a painful, itchy rash. Scratching the area spreads the rash—thus, it is important, though virtually impossible, to stop your toddler from scratching. Apply a hydrocortisone cream and cover the affected area with a dry cloth or bandage to limit the spread of the rash. Additionally, deliver a dose of diphenhydramine to the toddler to treat the itchiness. Consult your service provider as necessary.

Strep Throat

Strep throat is a highly contagious infection common in toddlers—particularly in those units who attend day care or preschool on a regular basis. Symptoms of strep throat include fever, sore throat, headache, abdominal pain, and/or rash. This infection must be treated by your toddler's service provider, who may perform a throat swab test to diagnose the condition. The service provider will most likely prescribe a course of antibiotics to treat the infection. Though a sore throat makes it difficult for your toddler to eat and drink, it is all the more important to keep your toddler hydrated.

Frequent recurrences of strep throat (four to six times per year) coupled with snoring or sleep apnea may require the removal of your unit's tonsils. Consult your service provider.

Swallowed/Nosed Objects

Unless an owner witnesses a toddler swallow an object or put objects up his nose, it may remain lodged for an extended time. Watch for and treat each condition in the following manner.

■ **Swallowed objects.** If your toddler has difficulty swallowing or breathing, follow the procedure to stop your toddler from choking (see page 188) and then visit the hospital immediately. Other indications that your toddler has swallowed an inappropriate object include vomiting or abdominal pain. In this instance, consult your toddler's service provider, who may recommend an X-ray to track the object's progress out of your toddler's system.

■ **Nosed objects.** Nosed objects are generally easier to diagnose than swallowed objects. If you witness your toddler sticking an object up his nose, encourage him to snort or blow it out into a tissue or hanky. If you notice unilateral drainage (from one side) of your toddler's nose coupled with an unpleasant odor, consult your service provider for proper removal.

[Appendix]

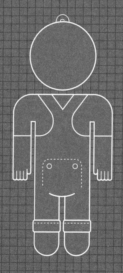

Toileting Diary

Name of Model

DAY	07:00 A.M.	07:30 A.M.	08:00 A.M.	08:30 A.M.	09:00 A.M.	09:30 A.M.	10:00 A.M.	10:30 A.M.	11:00 A.M.	11:30 A.M.	12:00 P.M.	12:30 P.M.	01:00 P.M.
SUN.													
MON.													
TUE.													
WED.													
THUR.													
FRI.													
SAT.													

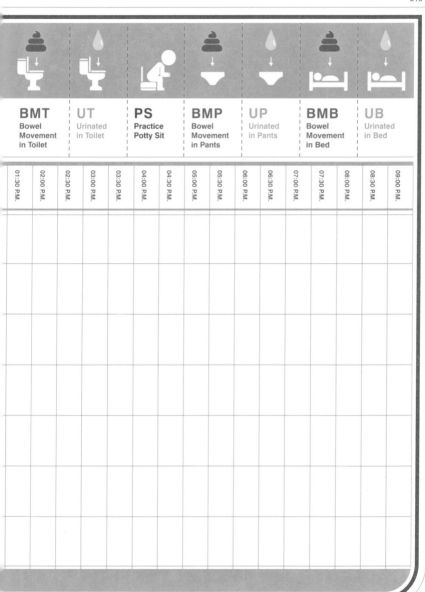

BMT Bowel Movement in Toilet	UT Urinated in Toilet	PS Practice Potty Sit	BMP Bowel Movement in Pants	UP Urinated in Pants	BMB Bowel Movement in Bed	UB Urinated in Bed

01:30 P.M.	02:00 P.M.	02:30 P.M.	03:00 P.M.	03:30 P.M.	04:00 P.M.	04:30 P.M.	05:00 P.M.	05:30 P.M.	06:00 P.M.	06:30 P.M.	07:00 P.M.	07:30 P.M.	08:00 P.M.	08:30 P.M.	09:00 P.M.

TODDLER'S SLEEP CHART		SUN.	MON.	TUE.	WED.	THUR.	FRI.	SAT.
★	11:30 P.M.							
	11:00 P.M.							
	10:30 P.M.							
	10:00 P.M.							
★	09:30 P.M.							
	09:00 P.M.							
	08:30 P.M.							
★	08:00 P.M.							
	07:30 P.M.							
★	07:00 P.M.							
	06:30 P.M.							
	06:00 P.M.							
	05:30 P.M.							
	05:00 P.M.							
	04:30 P.M.							
	04:00 P.M.							
	03:30 P.M.							
	03:00 P.M.							
	02:30 P.M.							
	02:00 P.M.							
	01:30 P.M.							
	01:00 P.M.							
	12:30 P.M.							
	12:00 P.M.							
	11:30 A.M.							
	11:00 A.M.							
	10:30 A.M.							
	10:00 A.M.							
	09:30 A.M.							
	09:00 A.M.							
	08:30 A.M.							
	08:00 A.M.							
	07:30 A.M.							
	07:00 A.M.							
	06:30 A.M.							
	06:00 A.M.							
	05:30 A.M.							
	05:00 A.M.							
	04:30 A.M.							
	04:00 A.M.							
	03:30 A.M.							
	03:00 A.M.							
★	02:30 A.M.							
	02:00 A.M.							
	01:30 A.M.							
★	01:00 A.M.							
	12:30 A.M.							
★	12:00 A.M.							

Index